Give Peace a Chance

A CATALOG OF THE EXHIBITION AT THE PEACE MUSEUM, CHICAGO

Give Peace a Chance

MUSIC AND THE STRUGGLE FOR PEACE

CHICAGO REVIEW PRESS   CHICAGO   ILLINOIS   60610

MARIANNE PHILBIN

EDITOR

DEDICATION BY

YOKO ONO

Cover Credits

Cover: front, from top—photo of U2 by Paul Natkin; poster, "From Vietnam Veterans to the World: A Night of Peace and Healing" (Vietnam Veterans Project); manuscript, "The Word," John Lennon and Paul McCartney (Northwestern University Libary); photo of Bob Marley by Bob Gruen, Radius Graphics; program for Peace Sunday (Lisa Law); photo of Bob Dylan and Joan Baez, taken at Peace Sunday, by Henry Diltz (Museum of Rock Art). Back cover—photo of John Lennon and Yoko Ono by Bob Gruen, Radius Graphics; manuscript for Joan Baez' "Cambodia"; sheet music, "The Letter That Never Reached Home," 1915. Photography of documents and solarization effects by Ken Todd.

Contents

Library of Congress 83-15117

ISBN 0-914091-35-2

All rights reserved.
Printed in the United States of America
First Edition
Published by Chicago Review Press
213 West Institute Place
Chicago, Illinois 60610

Cover photos: Bob Marley, John Lennon and Yoko Ono by Bob Gruen,
Radius Gallery, New York: Joan Baez and Bob Dylan by Henry Diltz;
U2 by Paul Natkin.

Dove logo for The Peace Museum by Bobbie Bluestein.

Exhibition Floor Plan rendering, p. 98, by Muller & Brown, Cincinnati.
Photography by Ken Todd.

Text designed by Arlene J. Sheer, Ampersand Book Design & Production, Chicago.
Text composition by Better Graphics, Inc., Crystal Lake, Illinois.
Display composition by J. M. Bundscho, Inc., Chicago.

To my family

I love you—if it were only for sharing this time of incredible challenge and great hope: the dawning of the age of peace. I know we'll make it. As our friend said, "There are no problems, only solutions."

I SEE RAINBOWS

It's getting cold around here
People living in fear
Whether it's a country or an island
Frighten by death
Holding our breath
While our souls cry out

I don't wanna be mugged by some mother
I don't wanna be shot for ten dollar
What's this talk about limited holocaust
Have a heart, I don't even want my roof to leak

I see rainbows
I see tomorrow
I see us sending rainbow love
I see rainbows
I see tomorrow
I see us sending rainbow thoughts

I don't wanna be part of terrorists
I don't wanna be one of survivalists
This is our world and it's beautiful
I wanna survive survive survive together

I see rainbows
I see tomorrow
I see us sending rainbow love
I see rainbow
I see tomorrow
I see us sending rainbow thoughts

love, yoko

Yoko Ono
New York City
June 29, '83

Acknowledgments

When we first started working on this exhibition, I don't think any of us had any idea how massive the project would eventually become. But as the project grew, so did the support we received from hundreds of people.

Special thanks go first and foremost to Mark Rogovin, who started it all, never slowed down and already can't wait to jump into the next exhibition; and to Marjorie Benton, who made us believe that we could do anything. Both Mark and Marjorie have an ability to see unlimited potential in what others might mistake for limited resources, the resources in this case being a few people and a good idea. It is because of their extraordinary vision, drive and committment that an institution like The Peace Museum exists at all, and that an exhibition like *Give Peace a Chance* can be presented.

Special thanks also go to Yoko Ono, whose early support helped make this exhibition a reality. Over a period of almost an entire year, Ms. Ono and her staff gave generously of their time and energy, suggesting possibilities, supplying information, and gathering materials. I am especially grateful to Sam Havadtoy and George Speerin for their gracious help and encouragement.

Working with our initial ideas and taking them a step further, Cincinnati architects Paul Muller and Terry Brown designed the exhibit. Paul and Terry devoted thousands of hours to this project, overseeing everything from the floor plan to lighting to graphics on the wall. I am indebted to them for guiding me through many difficult decisions and for contributing their enormous talent to the design of the exhibition.

Chief carpenters John Kesslering and Patrick Nelson turned the plans and sketches into walls and floors and ceilings, creating galleries as beautiful as the architects envisioned. John and Pat worked ten-hour days and supervised a crew of more than thirty volunteer carpenters and cabinet-makers, working in an un-airconditioned space where temperatures sometimes rose as high as 105°. Quite simply, without their help, the exhibit could never have opened.

There would have been little on the walls when the exhibit opened had it not been for the help I received from curatorial assistants Ruth Barrett and John Nawn. I could list hundreds of adjectives and still not even come close to describing how hard they worked and how much I came to depend on them. They were creative in the pursuit of even the strangest leads, calm under pressure, and organized to the last. In short, they never let me down.

Special thanks also go to Kerry Cochrane for her skilled research and fine writing, for seeing exactly what was needed and producing it; to Susan O'Brien for taking a leave of absence from her advertising agency and working full-time for us on publicity and promotions; to Sharon Queen for coordinating the volunteer program; Martin Moy for managing the museum store; to Sidney Schonberger, Charles Thomas, Paul Nebenzahl and Paul Murphy, for somehow managing to make a very little go a very long way; to Jennifer Hill, Mary Anne Wolff, Lu Ann Lewandowski, Charlotte Kaufman and Eric Krystall for special projects; and to our board of directors for their support.

Consultant Terri Hemmert of WXRT Radio became an honorary Peace Museum staffer during the last six months of preparations, working as long and as hard as we did, and jumping into new projects with the kind of enthusiasm and energy that helped keep everyone going. Terri contributed to many aspects of the exhibition, helping with research, acquisitions, promotion and special events.

Equally helpful was consultant Dottie Jeffries, museum store manager at The Museum of Science and Industry. Dottie steered us through what was for us uncharted territory, advising us on special merchandising and the ins-and-outs of setting up a museum store.

Expert advice and long hours of labor were also provided by audio-visual specialist John Boesche, who produced a fantastic slide

4

show for the rock room; and sound engineer Mark Guncheon, who filled the galleries with music.

I would also like to extend a special thank-you to Jann S. Wenner, editor and publisher of *Rolling Stone*. Jann provided not only valuable advice at the early stages of planning, he also provided valuable materials for the exhibition itself. He and assistant Mary McDonald helped us find our way through the maze of the music industry, putting us in touch with the right people at the right places.

Also helpful were Paul and Robin Caruso at The Museum of Rock Art in Hollywood. Paul and Robin were gracious hosts in L.A., and went out of their way to help me track down materials relative to West Coast musicians. Thanks as well go to photographers Lisa Law, Jan Butchofsky and Henry Diltz in Los Angeles, and Bob Gruen and Tom Wiener in New York.

In Chicago, photographer Paul Natkin was spectacularly helpful, an organizer extraordinaire. Thanks are due as well to Danny Narducy and Gregg Kincaid, Park West and Jam Productions; Jim Hirsch and Rebecca Shepard at the Old Town School of Folk Music; folk singer and folk historian Fred Holstein; Kate Fagan and Heavy Manners, Aaron Freeman and Crosscurrents; and Robert O'Connell of Yesterday's Party, all of whom contributed their time and talents to special events surrounding the opening of the exhibition.

As is always the case with projects of this magnitude, there are literally hundreds of people to thank, and unfortunately, never space enough to do so. Of all the volunteers who donated time, however, I would like to single out a few who have worked with us for more than a year: photographer Joseph Denov, a man of extraordinary dedication who has worked tirelessly on countless projects; Phil Berkman and Lyn Warren of the Museum of Contemporary Art; Donna Caplin, Rick Dalmar, Theresa Donnelly, Dan Gilman, Patty Kukla, Marcus Lawrence, Billy Natkin, Steve Pietsch, Mark Shelly, Rick Steinberg, Sherry Wier and Pat Piasecki.

I'd also like to thank Bonnie Bluestein, Randee Ladden and Mike Yanoff of The Peace Guild for graphic design work; Ronna Hoffberg at Rose Records; Laurie Sabol at the Chicago Public Library; and V.J. McAleer at NBC.

Lastly and perhaps most importantly, I would like to express my deepest gratitude and appreciation to all the musicians, all the managers, friends and families who helped to create this exhibition;

especially Joan Baez, Manny Greenhill, Nancy Lutzow, Diamonds
and Rust Productions; Holly Near, Melissa Howden, Redwood
Records; Bono Vox, Adam Clayton, The Edge, Larry Mullen,
Ellen Darst, Island Records; Graham Nash, Mac Holbert, Rudy
Records; Stevie Wonder, Marsha Smith, Black Bull Music; Pete
Seeger and Harold Leventhal; Country Joe McDonald and Florence
McDonald; Sandy Chapin; Mike Ochs; Laura Nyro; Randy New-
man and Donald Passman; Laurie Anderson; Tom Lehrer; Tom
Paxton, Craig Hankensen, Producers Inc.; Vern Partlow; Ruth
Burnstein, Nancy Schimmel, Schroder Music; and Gil Scott-Heron
and Chris Williams.

I'm also grateful to Chicago Review Press, and the wonderfully
patient Mary Munro.

Marianne Philbin
Curator
The Peace Museum

Introduction

MARIANNE PHILBIN

ALL OF THE MUSICIANS featured in this exhibition have at one time or another found themselves on a certain kind of tightrope. On this tightrope, Woody Guthrie was fearless; he scarcely seemed to notice its danger. John Lennon's audacity was different; he seemed virtually able to sleep while on it. For those of us who are more faint of heart, however, the problem is just to walk on it. This tightrope is the perch of the creative musician who would reveal in song a voice out of tune with a nation's war-like ways.

When we began planning more than a year ago to feature some of these tightrope walkers in an exhibition, we had little idea what we were getting into. We knew what we wanted to do: we wanted to create an exhibition on music and peace that would explore the history and celebrate the music. We wanted to highlight the contributions of some of the many musicians who had helped to promote peace, either through the music they created or through the campaigns they initiated and inspired.

Before we really got started, I think we naively hoped to find "music" and "peace" neatly cross-indexed in all the proper reference books, peace songs carefully listed in compendiums, memorabilia collected in archives. Instead, what we found was that the topics we were exploring had never been approached in quite this way before, and that there was a vast amount of material to uncover.

Marianne Philbin is Curator at The Peace Museum, Chicago.

This exhibit focuses on leading folk and rock musicians, but there are countless others who have spoken out through music, some who are perhaps lesser known like Charlie King; Si Kahn or Rev. Frederick Douglass Kirkpatrick, and others who represent areas not even touched by this exhibition, such as religious music, classical music, jazz, and blues.

This exhibit is by no means a comprehensive study of the history of peace music. It does not tell a story that ends. One of the most exciting aspects of putting together *Give Peace a Chance* was finding that it was impossible to keep up with new music, with all the ways in which musicians today are addressing peace issues. Music will continue to play a major role in inspiring efforts for peace as new musicians step onto the tightrope, taking real risks for the sake of conscience.

It's not easy to voice unpopular opinions, especially when your voice is being heard by thousands, and amplified untold times by the media. Consider Pete Seeger and The Weavers, who were blacklisted in the '50s for the "unamerican" content of their music. Consider Yoko Ono and John Lennon, whose bed-in for peace prompted one reporter to declare that Lennon had "come perilously near to having gone off his rocker." Or consider Frank Zappa, who severed relations with his record label when it refused to issue his single "I Don't Wanna Get Drafted." These musicians were risking not only financial security, but were stepping out of roles created for them by the record-buying public, and taking on new roles—many of which were confusing to and unpopular with their fans. Why flaunt political consciousness when it's struggle enough to make popular music? Why risk losing an audience by taking a side or speaking too loudly?

The musicians who succeed in maintaining a balance on the tightrope are not left alone there to relish their equilibrium. Lyricists are charged with forcing their views on their audience, reducing listeners to a chorus of mindless assent. If lyrics are too ambiguous, the writer is charged with conveying meaning while not taking responsibility for the message. The musician who overcomes these accusations and remains on his feet is sometimes said to be merely cashing in or selling out.

John Lennon and Yoko Ono were often accused of using peace as a way of getting free publicity. They were criticized for their bed-ins—turning their honeymoon into a press conference, giving statements to the media about the need for peace in the world.

They received, as they knew they would, huge amounts of publicity. And for that week, instead of our television screens and newspaper headlines being filled with stories of war and violence, we heard the Lennons telling us that "War is over, if you want it." This media blitz gave many the opportunity to attack the already controversial couple, it gave others the opportunity to ridicule them, and it allowed all of us to hear their very clear and simple message—a plea to "give peace a chance."

As we consider the ways in which music-makers have spoken to us about peace, we should remember that they could have chosen to avoid these questions altogether. It has in the past proven easier for tightrope walkers to become cynical and lose sight of their reasons for staying up there. The purpose of this exhibition is not simply to tell the history of those of our heroes and heroines who became masters of the tightrope, but to achieve in some small way what John, Yoko and all the others tried to accomplish with their campaigns—to bring peace issues and concerns into the limelight, to fill the senses of an audience with the music and message of peace, and to encourage that audience to do what they can within their own lives to give peace that chance.

Give Peace a Chance: An Anthem for the Anti-War Movement

JON WIENER

JOHN LENNON AND YOKO ONO married in March, 1969, moved into the Amsterdam Hilton for their honeymoon, and announced that a happening was about to take place in their bed. Holland was permissive, but the chief of Amsterdam's vice squad issued a stern warning: "If people are invited to such a 'happening,' the police would certainly act." Fifty newspeople crowded outside their hotel room. "These guys were sweating to fight to get in first because they thought we were going to be making love in bed. That's where their minds were at," John later recalled. "How could they think that?" Yoko asked. "Because we'd been naked: naked, bed, John and Yoko, sex." When the newsmen entered, John and Yoko were sitting in bed, wearing pajamas. "I hope it's not a let-down," John said. "We wouldn't make love in public—that's an emotionally personal thing."

He announced that they would stay in bed for a week, "our protest against all the suffering and violence in the world." They conducted interviews ten hours a day, starting at ten in the morning. John explained, "We're sending out a message, mainly to youth, or to anybody interested in protesting against any form of violence. . . . Things like the Grovesnor Square marches in London, the end product of it all was just newspaper stories about riots and fighting. We did the bed-in in Amsterdam . . . just to give people the idea that there are many ways of protest. . . .

The interviewer went on to ask, "If anything happened to you, how would you like to be remembered?" John took the question as referring to both of them: "As the great peaceniks," he replied. "That before your music?" Without hesitation: "Oh sure."

Copyright 1983 by Jon Wiener. Excerpted from *"Give Me Some Truth": John Lennon and the Sixties,* to be published by Random House in the spring of 1984.

Jon Wiener teaches history at the University of California at Irvine.

11

Photograph of John Lennon and Yoko Ono by
Bob Gruen, 1975 (Bob Gruen, Radius Graphics)

Protest for peace in any way, but peacefully, 'cause we think
that peace is only got by peaceful methods, and that to fight the
establishment with their own weapons is no good because they
always win, and they've been winning for thousands of years.
They know how to play the game of violence. But they don't
know how to handle humor, and peaceful humor—and that's our
message really."

The establishment press was outraged by the bed-in. Particularly in the London press, John and Yoko received a torrent of
abuse. "This must rank as the most self-indulgent demonstration of

all time," one columnist wrote. Another commented that John "seems to have come perilously near to having gone off his rocker." Even Beatle fans expressed a sense of betrayal.

Yoko defended the Bed-Ins on the grounds of the impracticality of other forms of protest for them. "We can't go out in Trafalgar Square because it would create a riot," she said. "We can't lead a parade or a march because of all the autograph hunters. We had to find our own way of doing it, and for now Bed-Ins seem the most logical way."

But if the Bed-Ins seemed to combine a whimsical pacifism with a necessary practicality, in fact they had a much more serious and radical basis. Yoko in particular was drawing on her background as an artist to bring together avant-garde performance art with radical politics. She was seeking to overcome the apolitical and anti-political aspects of avant-garde art in a way that would also liberate radical political activity from its traditional forms, especially the protest march.

The bed-in also represented an early exercise in New Left media politics. John and Yoko rejected the view, held by many in the anti-war movement, that the newspapers and TV were necessarily and exclusively instruments of corporate domination of popular consciousness. They sought to work within the mass media to undermine their basis, to use them, briefly and sporadically, against the system in which they functioned. This project had obvious dangers. But it represented a bold effort to break out of the insularity of the older peace movement; it was based a commitment to reach a completely new audience with radical politics; and it expressed a seriousness in grappling with new cultural forms whose power over popular thinking was undeniably great.

Those who questioned the "effectiveness" of the bed-in missed part of its significance. Liberals consistently criticized the anti-war movement for being "ineffective," asserting that effective leaders worked for changes within the system. John and Yoko, along with the counterculture and the New Left, rejected that conception. They considered respectable, routine politics to be part of the problem. To attack the conventions of ordinary politics, to undermine its forms, itself had radical significance. By staying in bed for a week to protest the war, by "doing their own thing," John and Yoko were rejecting the liberal conception of political effectiveness.

Yoko explained how they felt after the bed-in. "Because people kept saying we were crazy, we went into a very, very deep depres-

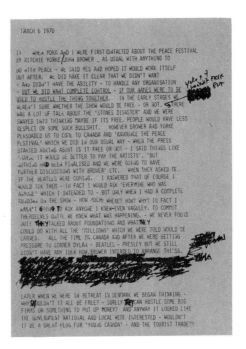

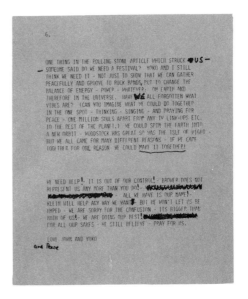

Letter from John Lennon and Yoko Ono to *Rolling Stone* regarding their involvement in the Toronto Peace Festival, typed with handwritten notations, March 6, 1970, 8½″ × 11″ (Jann S. Wenner)

sion. We thought, 'Oh well, they were right. We didn't do very much. And it didn't help the world.' We were very sad, because there was no response.

"But then we started to get a tremendous, beautiful response around the end of the year. And that gave us hope." John explained, "For instance some guy wrote 'now, because of your event in Amsterdam, I'm not joining the RAF, I'm growing my hair.'" A skeptical interviewer asked whether staying in bed meant anything, even as a symbol. "Imagine if the American army stayed in bed for a week," John replied. But, the interviewer persisted, wouldn't it be better if people "went out and did something?" "If you say you can do better than that, do it," John said. "Go ahead and top us!"

The interviewer went on to ask, "If anything happened to you, how would you like to be remembered" John took the question as referring to both of them: "As the great peaceniks," he replied. "That before your music?" Without hesitation: "Oh sure."

John and Yoko decided to bring their peace campaign to the U.S. where it really belonged. But Nixon immigration officials refused John's request for an entry visa—the first blow in what would become a protracted war lasting from 1972 to 1975. John and Yoko announced plans for a bed-in in the Soviet Union; "it's easier to get into Russia than the U.S.," he complained. They settled on Montreal as the city closest to the U.S. media to stage their second bed-in for peace, arrived in May, 1969, and did more than 60 radio interviews.

In their most radical act in the Montreal bed-in, John and Yoko welcomed an American army deserter to their bedside. Introduced as a 22-year-old from "Boston and the Fort Dix stockade," he brought his wife and six-month-old daughter. He came as a member of the American Deserters Committee, one of fifty deserters who Canada legally admitted. The deserter explained to John and the assembled media, "We were told by the system to go and kill."

"I'm sympathetic," John replied. "The only way we can change the system is to do it nonviolently. . . . Gandhi's way," he said.

A reporter picked up on that point: "should the U.S. have come to Britain's aid in 1941, when Hitler threatened?"

"What happened then was right for that moment," John replied.

The last night of the Montreal bed-in John taught everyone in the room the new song he had written, and recorded it on an eight-track portable tape recorder he had installed. On John's first non-Beatles recording, the back-up singers were Yoko, Dick Gregory,

14

Timothy Leary, Tommy Smothers, Murray the K, Petula Clark, a rabbi, a priest, and the Canadian chapter of the Radha Krishna temple. The song, the musical product of the bed-ins, was "Give Peace a Chance."

Released a single in the U.S. in July, 1969, the song reached number 14 on the American charts in September and number two on the British charts. It received top-40 radio play for nine weeks, and became a million-seller worldwide.

John sang the song with a cheerful enthusiasm; it bounced along over rich cross-rhythms. And he sang verses filled with words, apparently whimsical nonsense lyrics: "everybody's talking 'bout madism, bagism, shagism, dragism." On closer examination, the song had clear politics. John's verses called on people to put aside

Bed-In in Montreal, 1969, Photo by Roy Kerwood.

15

political differences and factionalism within the antiwar movement, to unite around the simple demand for "peace." John treated political positions as "isms":

> Everybody's talking 'bout . . .
> This-ism, that-ism, ism-ism-ism.
> All we are saying
> Is give peace a chance.
> Revolution, evolution . . .
> United nations, congratulations,
> All we are saying . . .

In his 1968 song "Revolution," on the Beatles' White Album, John had explicitly opposed those who took a revolutionary position. Here he simply called on them to put aside their political differences with liberals. If the apolitical character of the song aroused opposition from the left, it also contributed to the song's success in a peace movement that itself tended to avoid deeper political questions. As Pete Seeger said, "Undoubtedly some people wanted to say a lot more than 'give peace a chance.' On the other hand, history gets made when people come to the same conclusion from many different directions. And this song did hit a common denominator. There's no doubt about it."

The credits on the Apple single of "Give Peace a Chance" are strange. For the first time, John wrote and sang on a record without the Beatles. But his did not take credit as performer. He gave that to "Plastic Ono Band." His name appears twice: as co-producer, with Yoko; and as co-author, with Paul McCartney. Paul did not co-author the song, but John was sticking with the agreement, made almost a decade earlier, that any song written by either would be credited to "Lennon-McCartney." That credit on "Give Peace a Chance" suggested that John was not quite ready to break up the Beatles. But it made a significant statement about the impending break-up: to leave the Beatles was to join the anti-war movement.

October 1, 1969, demonstrators held the first of a new series of protests, *Vietnam Moratorium Day.*" Millions of people demonstrated in cities and towns across the country. Organizers explained that these local protests were a prelude to a gigantic demonstration to be held in Washington, D.C. the next month. Nixon sent Agnew to respond as he had in the past. The vice-president said anti-war demonstrators were "encouraged by an effete corps of impudent snobs who characterize themselves as intellectuals." Impudent snobs picketing the White House and on the steps of St.

Single (first issue) "Give Peace a Chance" by John Lennon. Produced by John Lennon, Yoko Ono, and The Plastic Ono Band, recorded during the Bed-In For Peace, Hotel La Reine Elizabeth, Montreal. © Northern Songs, Ltd, 1969, 7¼" × 7¼" (J. V. McShirley)

16

Patrick's Cathedral in New York sang the new song: "Give Peace a Chance." "The organizers of the marches did not promote the song," one observer commented. "It just happened."

On November 15, Vietnam Moratorium Day was declared in Washington D.C. Pete Seeger led around half a million demonstrators singing John's song at the Washington Monument—while Richard Nixon sat in the White House with Bebe Rebozo, watching football on TV. Pete Seeger recalled that day. "I guess I faced the biggest audience I've ever faced in my entire life," he said. "Hundreds of thousands, how many I don't know. They stretched as far as the eye could see up the hillside and over the hill. I'd only heard the song myself a few days before, and I confess when I first heard it I didn't think much of it. I thought 'That's kind of a nothing of a song, it doesn't go anyplace.' I heard a young woman sing it at a peace rally. I never heard his record. I didn't know if the people there had ever heard it before. But I decided to try singing it over and over again, until they did know it.

"Well, we started singing, and after a minute or so I realized it was still growing. Peter, Paul and Mary jumped up and started joining in. A couple of more minutes, and Mitch Miller hops up on the stage and starts waving his arms. I realized it was getting better and better. The people started swaying their bodies and banners and flags in time, several hundred thousand people, parents with their small children on their shoulders. It was a tremendously moving thing."

Later interviewers asked John what he had thought about that day. He explained, "I'm shy and aggressive, so I have great hopes for what I do with my work and I also have great despair. . . . I got through all that, and in me secret heart I wanted to write something that would take over "We Shall Overcome.' . . . I thought, why doesn't somebody write one for the people now. That's what my job is, our job is."

And in another interview, he recalled, "I saw pictures of that Washington demonstration on British TV, with all those people singing it, forever and not stopping. . . . It was one of the biggest moments of my life." He was right to be proud. As *Newsweek* proclaimed in an article on the song, "The peace movement had found an anthem."

The Press Conference: John Lennon and Yoko Ono Talk about Peace

There are a lot of people around the world now trying to promote world peace. Why do you think that you can succeed where they have so far failed?

That's like saying why bother keeping on Christianity because Jesus got killed. We don't think people have tried advertising before. Pretend peace is new then 'cause we've never had it. So you start advertising it: . . . Sell, sell, sell.

Are there any similarities between where the Beatles were during the Cavern days and this peace campaign now?

We do consider that we're in the Cavern stage; you know, we haven't got out of Liverpool with this campaign. And we've got to break London and then America. I feel exactly the same as I did then about the Beatles as I do about peace and what we're doing now. But I don't care how long it takes, and what obstacles there are. We won't stop.

Was there any one incident that got you into the peace campaign?

Well, it built up over a number of years, but the thing that struck it off was a letter we got from a guy called Peter Watkins, who made a film called *The War Game*. It was a long letter stating what's happening—how the media is controlled, how it's run, and it ended up: "What are you going to do about it?"

You either get tired fighting for peace, or you die.

From a 1970 press conference. Reprinted by permission from *Rolling Stone*.

He said people in our position and his position have a responsibility to use the media for world peace. And we sat on the letter for three weeks and thought it over and figured at first we were doing our best with songs like "All You Need Is Love."

Finally we came up with the bed event and that was what sparked it off. It was like getting your call-up papers for peace. Then we did the bed event.

Is it true you were planning on going to Biafra a short while back?

Yeah. At the time, Yoko was pregnant and we decided not to go and she had a miscarriage. Then we thought and thought about it. But we're scared to go somewhere where it's happening. 'Cause we don't want to be dead saints or martyrs. I'm scared of going to Vietnam and Biafra and, until I'm convinced that I can do better there than I can do outside of it, I'll stay out of it. I'd go to Russia, but I'd think twice about China.

YOKO: I think we did a lot of good for Biafra when John returned his M.B.E.

You said you were going to have a peace vote. How do you answer accusations that that sort of thing borders on naiveté?

Let's see. If anybody thinks our campaign is naive, that's their opinion and that's okay. Let them do something else and if we like their ideas, we'll join in with them. But until then, we'll do it the way we are. We're artists, not politicians. Not newspapermen, not anything. We do it in the way that suits us best, and this is the way we work.

Publicity and things like that is our game. The Beatles' thing was that. And that was the trade I've learned. This is my trade, and I'm using it to the best of my ability.

But what is the point of having a vote for peace?

Why do people have those Gallup polls? If we get a vote from around the world with millions and millions of kids that want peace, that's a nice Gallup poll. We can wave those figures around. That's all. It's a positive move; all we want is a yes.

Will the Beatles play at this festival?

I'll try to hustle them out. Maybe I'll get on two of them, or something like that. I got George on the other night for UNICEF in London. I can't speak for the Beatles because I'm only me. But if

Poster, *War Is Over If You Want It,*
30½" × 20½" (Yoko Ono)

I can get them, if I can get Elvis . . . I'll try. I'll try and get all of them.

Do you think this festival could become something like that recent Stones affair in California, where some people died?

The Stones' one was bad. I've heard a lot of things about that concert. I think it was just a bad scene. It won't be like that here. I think they created that either subconsciously or whatever, and that is the result of the image and the mood they create. I think if you create a peaceful scene, you stand a better chance. We have six months to prevent that sort of thing; the Stones thing was done overnight.

How soon can the world reach a state of peace?

As soon as people realize that they have the power. The power doesn't belong with Mr. Trudeau, Mr. Wilson or Mr. Nixon. We are the power. The people are the power. And as soon as people are aware that they have the power, then they can do what they want. And if it's a case of they don't know what to do, let's advertise to them to tell them they have an option. They've all got a vote. Vote for peace, folks.

Don't you think your long hair and your clothes may put old people off in your pursuit of peace?

I understand that. Many people say, "Why don't you get a butch haircut and a tie, suit?" and the thing is, that's what politicians do. We just try to be as natural as possible. Now, how many members of the public are gullible to politicians, with the nice picture of the family, the dog and the whore on the side? Now, I could do that, but I don't think people would believe it. That's the politicians' way, but youth certainly doesn't believe it anymore.

Have you ever thought of taking your ideas to someone like Henry Ford?

When we get a bit organized. You see, what we didn't want to become was leaders. I believe in that Wilhelm Reich guy who said, "Don't become a leader." We don't want to be the people that everyone says, "It was your fault we didn't get peace." We want to be part of it. It's like people said the Beatles were the movement; but we were only part of the movement. We were influenced as much as we influenced.

John Lennon, photograph by Bob Gruen, 1975
(Bob Gruen, Radius Graphics)

And John and Yoko refuse to be the leaders of the youth movement for peace. That's dictatorship. We want everybody to help us. And then, if it takes time for this kind of news to get through to Henry Ford or Onassis or anybody like that.

When we get something functional happening and a few people that aren't John and Yoko, we can approach from that angle. We can then say we've got so much money, will you double it? 'Cause we know they all do charity for whatever reason.

Do you believe in God?

Yes, I believe that God is like a powerhouse, like where you keep electricity, like a power station. And that he's a supreme power, and that he's neither good nor bad, left, right, black or white. He just is. And we tap that source of power and make of it what we will. Just as electricity can kill people in a chair, or you can light a room with it. I think God is.

Don't you worry about being identified as a father figure?

I believe that leaders and father figures are the mistake of all the generations before us. And that all of us rely on Nixon or Jesus or whoever we rely on; it's lack of responsibility that you expect somebody else to do it. He must help me or we kill him or we vote

John Lennon and Yoko Ono (Bob Gruen, Radius Graphics)

him out. I think that's the mistake, just having father figures. It's a sign of weakness; you must do the greasing yourself.

I won't be a leader. Everybody is a leader. People thought the Beatles were leaders, but they weren't, and now people are finding that out.

What, in brief, is your philosophy?

Peace, just no violence, and everybody grooving, if you don't mind the word. Of course, we all have violence in us, but it must be channeled or something. If I have long hair, I don't see why everybody else should have long hair. And if I want peace, I'll suggest peace to everyone. But I won't hustle them up for peace.

If people want to be violent, let them not interfere with people who don't want violence. Let them kill each other if there has to be that.

Are there any alternatives?

You either get tired fighting for peace, or you die.

Don't you think the Peace Grease may be a substitute for the massive problem young people are having with drugs?

Well, the liquor problem is even worse. I think the drug problem is a hang-up and a drag, but if we hadn't had methedrine, and all the rest of it, the ones that are going to go through that trip

John Lennon and Yoko Ono walking in Central Park in 1980, shortly before Lennon's death. This area of Central Park was later named "Strawberry Fields" in Lennon's honor by the City of New York. (Wide World Photos, Inc.)

would have been alcoholics. Everybody seems to need something in the way society is; because of the pressure. So it would have been alcohol or something. The problem isn't what they're on, it's what made them go on whatever they're on.

The best antidote for drug taking and liquor is hope, it seems to me. You're giving young people hope.

The only time Yoko and I took heavy drugs was when we were without hope. And the only way we got out of it was with hope. And if we can sustain the hope, we don't need liquor, hard drugs, or anything. But if we lose hope, what can you do? What is there to do?

John, would you have achieved that hope without the success of the Beatles?

The Beatles had nothing to do with the hope. This is after; I mean, the Beatles made it four years ago and they stopped touring and they had all the money they wanted, and all the fame they wanted and they found out they had nothing. And then we started on our various trips of LSD and Maharishi and all the rest of the things we did. And the old gag about money and power and fame is not the answer. We didn't have any hope just because we were famous.

You see, Marilyn Monroe and all the other people, they had everything the Beatles had, but it's no answer. So John and Yoko had the same problems and fears and hopes and aspirations that any other couple on earth does, regardless of the position we were in and regardless of the money we had. We had exactly the same paranoia as everybody else, the same petty thoughts, the same everything. We had no superanswer that came through Beatles or power. In that respect, the Beatles were irrelevant to what I'm talking about.

Getting back to how it started, how did you and Yoko initially find ground for this campaign?

Both Yoko and I were in different bags, as we call it. But both had a positive side—we were singing. "All You Need Is Love" and she was in Trafalgar Square, protesting for peace in a black bag. We met, we had to decide what our common goal was, we had one thing in common—we were in love. But love is just a gift, and it doesn't answer everything and it's like a precious plant that you have to nurture and look after and all that.

John Lennon

Cartoon which appeared in the *Des Moines Register* after the death of John Lennon. Drawing by Frank Millard, 8½″ × 11″

24

So we had to find what we wanted to do together—these two egos. What they had in common was love; we had to work on it. What goes with love, we thought, was peace. Now we were thinking of all this, and planning on getting married and not getting married and what we were going to do and how we were going to do it and rock & roll and avant-garde and all that bit, and then we got that letter from Peter Watkins. And it all started from there.

Surrender
to Peace

YOKO ONO

JOHN AND I were part of the huge crowd of world youth who grew up believing in the American idealism and its claim for human rights. We lived in societies under lingering Victorian influence while sharing the American dream in our hearts. America was us: the navigator to the future world. John held his belief to the end.

The dream still lives. This is evident in the letters I receive from the world in sharp contrast to the prevailing pessimism here in the states. The world has witnessed American spirit rising with remarkable resilience when it's most needed and often when it's least expected. No doubt it will again. My concern is how. We don't need another martyr. We have had one too many.

Compare the two last times when the American spirit has surged to bring justice to and for the nation. One being the Vietnam peace movement and the other, the Watergate incident. No blame intended to any individual and group heroes, there was much painful bloodshed connected with the peace movement whereas there was none with Watergate. Heroes involved there were either silent or masked, and the incongruity of it was directly responsible to the unfolding of the case. I observed this as strong evidence of our growing awareness, that emotional radicalism is power play with emphasis on play, and peace nurtures peace as justice seeds justice. Sanity is allowing dichotomy, unity is discovering empathy, and harmony is a celebration of polarity. Our purpose is not to

The dream still lives.

This article first appeared as a paid advertisement in the *New York Times* January 24, 1983.

27

exert power but to express our need for unity despite the seemingly unconquerable differences. We as the human race have a history of losing our emotional equilibrium when we discover different thought patterns in others. Many wars have been fought as a result. It's about time to recognize that it is alright to be wearing different hats as our heartbeat is always one.

I would like to propose a nationwide peace poll to vote for peace versus nuclear holocaust of any size. The poll should be clearly independent from nuclear disarmament and/or gun control issues for now, as many of us feel a strong need for nuclear defense while regarding gun control a non-priority cause. Combining either or both of these issues with the peace poll would immediately reduce the poll to a minority venture. The poll should be authorized and organized by the congress as a national undertaking for the sake of expediency alone, with the balloting through the media to minimize administrative expense. What the peace poll will do is to 1) show us where we stand in terms of individual and collective commitment to world peace and 2) inspire the rest of the world to follow.

There may come a time, sooner than we imagine, when the world would feel safe to curtail production of nuclear arms. The cost cutback alone would be a direct financial gain to every country. Already some of us are starting to feel suspicious of the old myth that war is more lucrative than peace, especially after observing that the world's largest weapon merchant, U.S.A., has not been exempt from the world economic crisis.

One could say that because of the times the people of the United States and their government have been given an opportunity to initiate world peace. To take this initiative is to leave a tremendous legacy to our offspring, a legacy of our true concern for the future race and our planet. How can we ask our children to be caring when we ourselves show indifference to their fate? Smile to the future and it will smile back to us.

I pray that in the end gun control will cease to be an issue, as today's misuse of guns may be due to the world tension for fear calls fear. A day may come when we will see governments offering to buy private guns for recycling to, say, make domestic robots. A few guns perhaps would remain in museums next to the early American spears for example as reminders of days when we used to kill each other to put stop to our lives before our natural deaths. Would they ever understand how much sorrow was caused by this instrument and its ritual I wonder? The true motivation for murdering one's fellow human is and will be an eternal mystery to us.

In the beginning there was the Word. If the universe was initially created by a word and its air play of seven days, wouldn't it be a comparatively modest effort on our part to work together through affirmation and reaffirmation of our unity, to ensure the survival of our already existing planet? If, as we know now, all of us are only using less than 20% of our brains, it is not an exaggeration to say that our awareness knows no boundary, and a miracle is what we make of it.

The eighties has become the most unusually beautiful, enlightened period in the history of the human race. It is as though the very tension has forced us to wake up from the long embryonic period we held on to. We are witnessing a unique society where all our feelings and thoughts have been brought out to the surface to be shared and reexamined. Not only that we have become closer to each other and wiser, but the wiser have become meeker and the meeker have become wiser thus making us truly one world.

Yoko Ono, photographed by Bob Gruen, 1983 (Polygram Records)

In the summer of '72 in New York City, John and I invited the press to announce the founding of a conceptual country called Nutopia. Anybody could be a citizen of this country. Citizens were automatically the country's ambassadors. The country's body was the airfield of our joint thoughts. Its constitution was our love, and its spirit, our dreams. Its flag was the white flag of surrender. A surrender to peace. We wished that one day we would take the flag to the United Nations and place it alongside the other flags as Nutopia was just another concept, as were concepts such as France, United States, and the Soviet Union. It was not a concept founded to threaten any other. At the time, the idea of "surrender" did not go down too well. A radical friend of ours expressed that he, too, disliked the term. "Surrender sounds like defeat," he said. "Well, don't you surrender to love, for instance?", I looked at him. "No, he wouldn't," I thought. "Are women the only people who know the pride and joy of surrender?" I wondered. "It's a waste of time to explain to a macho radical, didn't I tell you?" said John, a man who surrendered to the world, life, and finally to universe. "Anyway, don't worry, Yoko. One day we'll put it up there. You and I. I promise." I still believe we will.

It is time for you to rise. It is you who will raise the flag. I feel that John and I, as a unit, have done our share. The rest of my life belongs to our son, Sean. It is your effort. Your flag. So remember,

29

we are family. You and I are unity. In the joy of harmony, the world is one to infinity. Speak out. Speak out of love and you need not fear. We will hear. America the beautiful. Surrender to peace. I love you. Yoko Ono Lennon December 25 '82 New York City.

P.S. Just now, I received a call that a friend, Jamie Lubarr was shot to death Christmas Eve. He was walking on the streets of New York to go to a party. Two people came from behind and shot him with no apparent reason.

I'm sorry, Jamie. It was too late for you, and for the approximately 24,000 sisters and brothers who were shot to death this year in U.S.A. Just with handguns alone (F.B.I. Unified Reported Crime Statistics, Washington, D.C.) From January to October '82. This means one every thirty minutes. The rising violence is a world phenomenon in varying shades of cruelty. Closing our eyes to it will not make it disappear.

I have not slept well since John died. One bedside light is always lit through the night. It is as though I have no right to sleep in the comfort of darkness. I have my moments of joy and laughter. Night is when I face myself, John, and the dreams we dreamt together. There is anger and sorrow. Still, gun for a gun is not the way. If we took that route, pretty soon, you would be hearing me say, "Well, thank God, we're alive. That's 'cause my son is such a good marksman." I don't want to live that way. Forget the moral implication for a moment. How do we sleep? There is always a better marksman somewhere.

So I say it again. Speak out. Speak out of the wisdom of love— through love we have the power to create heaven on earth as love is heaven and heaven is love. The man said, "Half of what I say is meaningless, but I say it just to reach you."

Love, Yoko

John Lennon
and the FBI

ROXANE ARNOLD

FBI AGENTS, FEARING that former Beatle John Lennon was about to lead a demonstration against Richard Nixon, followed the late British musician for months before the 1972 Republican convention, hoping to arrest him on drug charges or otherwise "neutralize" him so that he could be deported, according to previously unreleased government documents.

In a bizarre story of a widespread government effort to catch Lennon in some illegal activity, FBI agents monitored the singer's public appearances, kept tabs on his private life and strongly suggested at one point that Lennon "be arrested if at all possible on possession of narcotics charges" so "that he would become more likely to be immediately deportable."

Although no evidence exists of any Lennon plan to disrupt or even attend the political convention, the government's campaign was relentless, according to FBI and immigration files released under the U.S. Freedom of Information Act.

The files comprise a virtual log of Lennon's life in the early '70s, a time when his records like "Imagine" were selling in the millions, his rhetoric was increasingly antiwar and he was fighting deportation because of a minor marijuana arrest in England four years before.

Included in the FBI file are some of Lennon's more controversial

The files comprise a virtual log of Lennon's life in the early '70s, a time when . . . his rhetoric was increasingly antiwar.

anti-war song lyrics, flyers from peace marches he attended, concert reviews, copies of counter-culture publications that linked his name to then Democratic presidential candidate George McGovern, and copies of secret memos and FBI reports that were distributed to bureaus across the country. FBI director J. Edgar Hoover, White House special assistant H.R. Haldeman, immigration authorities, State Department officials and the CIA also received communications.

Requested by University of California, Irvine, history professor Jon Wiener for a book he is writing, on Lennon and the politics of the '60s, much of the FBI material that was released is heavily censored.

Entire passages are blocked out with heavy black ink for what the FBI calls national security reasons. Wiener also received 26 pounds of immigration data detailing Lennon's three-year-fight with immigration authorities to stay in the United States.

According to the files, the government first took serious note of Lennon as a potential security threat in late 1971 after he attracted 16,000 people to a University of Michigan rally to free political activist John Sinclair. Sentenced to 10 years in prison for selling two marijuana cigarettes to an undercover officer, Sinclair was freed two days later.

In the months afterwards, Lennon's name appeared regularly on FBI coded teletypes, secret memoranda and other investigation reports.

In early March, 1972, deportation proceedings were launched against him, allegedly because of his marijuana conviction in England. But subsequent press reports linked the move to deport Lennon to a Feb. 4, 1972, memo written to then Atty. Gen. John Mitchell by Republican Sen. Strom Thurmond of South Carolina. Thurmond, who headed the Senate's internal security subcommittee, suggested that "headaches might be avoided" if action was taken.

By then Lennon was listed on FBI documents along with anti-war activists Rennie Davis, Jerry Rubin and others who were going to "direct New Left protest activities during the 1972 election year." All, according to an FBI report, were associated with a group known as the Election Year Strategy Information Center (EYSIC). The group's purpose was to disrupt the Republican Convention, then scheduled for San Diego but eventually held in Miami.

Memo from John Lennon's F.B.I. file, released March, 1983, to Jon Wiener under the Freedom of Information Act, 8½" × 11" (Jon Wiener)

The confidential memos included a review of Lennon's TV appearance with Jerry Rubin on the Mike Douglas Show and the published lyrics of the song "John Sinclair." Some of the communications were distributed not only to domestic FBI bureaus but also to the Secret Service, the U.S. attorney's office and U.S. Naval investigators in San Diego. By March, the CIA joined the list receiving information on Lennon, according to the file.

In April, when legal maneuverings stalled Lennon's deportation, FBI Director Hoover asked agents to "be aware of his activities and movements.

"In view of subject's avowed intention to engage in disruptive activities surrounding (the convention), New York office will be responsible for closely following his activities until time of actual deportation," the FBI director wrote in an April 10 memorandum.

The memo noted that "John Lennon, former member of the Beatles singing group, is allegedly in the U.S. to assist in organizing disruption of the RNC . . . Strong possibility looms that subject will not be deported any time soon . . . "

An April 21 memo from an agent to Edward S. Miller, who headed the FBI's intelligence division, confirmed Lennon's moves were "being closely followed and any information developed indicating violation of federal laws" was to be sent to appropriate law enforcement officials to "neutralize" the singer.

Original cartoon drawing by Doug Marlette appearing in *The Charlotte Observer* following the release of John Lennon's F.B.I. files © King Features Syndicate 1983, pen and pencil on cardboard 14½″ × 23″ (Doug Marlette)

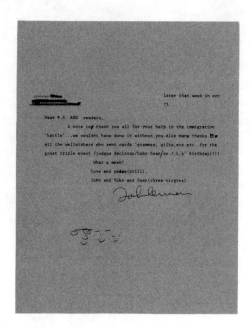

John Lennon's thank-you note to *Rolling Stone* readers after winning immigration battle, October 1975, typewritten on paper, 8½" × 11" (Jann S. Wenner)

With the August convention date nearing, the FBI again urged a possible Lennon drug bust.

The top New York agent suggested on July 27 that agents in Miami, where the Republican convention was to be held three weeks later, should be made aware of Lennon's drug use.

Lennon's drug history should also "be emphasized to local law enforcement agencies covering (the convention) with regards to subject being arrested if at all possible on narcotics charges."

The agent said if Lennon was arrested in Miami, his immediate deportation was likely.

But Lennon, by now mostly involved in fighting his deportation, never went to Miami.

Three years later, Lennon won his deportation battle when a U.S. appeals court in Manhattan ruled in his favor.

"What is most disturbing in all of this," historian Wiener said, "is the dimensions of what the government was doing. The government feared John Lennon, and Nixon devoted an incredible amount of government resources to try and get rid of him.

"What's even more disturbing than what they sent is what has been omitted. Of the 281-page file, 199 pages have been withheld in their entirety."

This Ain't No Foolin' Around: Giving Peace a Chance in the '80s

TERRI HEMMERT

ROCK MUSIC AND PEACE. Think of the '60s? Think again. In the past five years we've seen a renaissance of rock music delving into social concerns other than social disease and romance. If nothing else, Ronald Reagan and Margaret Thatcher have inspired some of the best songs since the '60s on economic chaos, political oppression, Orwellian fears of the future, the threat and reality of war, and the thirst for a true peace. But let's not give those two all of the credit for these great records. Juntas, generals and terrorists all over the world have served as deadly muses. Rock bands, artists and writers have rallied round the cause with song lyrics, video tapes, record cover art, and promotional items that reflect their growing concern.

The geography of peace songs in the '80s spans from Northern Ireland to Argentina, from Chile to Iran, from Poland to El Salvador, from Moscow to Washington.

There are few anthems in the '80s. Gone is the simple purity of "Give Peace a Chance." After all, we've been through a couple of decades of change. Debbie Harry sings on the Blondie song "English Boy,"

In 1969 I had a lousy time.
I listened to the songs, read letters sent from Nam.
Now peace and love are gone, the tired soldiers home.
Ideal society gunned down the '70s.

Terri Hemmert is a disk jockey and Public Affairs Director for WXRT radio in Chicago.

But we'll get to those changes later. There is some deja vu quality for those who remember doing the draft dodger rag in the '60s with Phil Ochs when they hear The Clash sing about draft resistance in "The Call Up":

It's up to you not to hear the call-up.
I don't wanna die.
It's up to you not to hear the call-up.
I don't wanna kill.
For he who will die is he who will kill.

Frank Zappa released a single entitled "I Don't Want to Get Drafted," and the Dead Kennedys agreed in "When Ya Get Drafted":

Are you believing the morning papers?
War is coming back in style.
There's generals here, advisors there, and Russians nibbling
    everywhere . . .
Economy is looking bad.
Let's start another war.

Some '60s history does show up in the new music, like in the Clash song "Washington Bullets."

The Bay of Pigs in 1961,
Havana for the playboys in the Cuban Sun.
For Castro is a color, is a redder than Red.
Those Washington bullets want Castro dead.

And there is the ghost of Vietnam. Passing references like John Cale's in "River Bank": "O Madame Nhu, yes madame knew." The Clash write in "Charlie Don't Surf," "Charlie's gonna be a napalm star." And the English Beat in "I Am Your Flag,"

Took your hat off in Wisconsin,
Took your head in Vietnam,
Just dying to become a man.
Well, I am your flag.

There are some holdovers from the '60's (let's not call them "war-horses"). Some of the rock and roll survivors are writing about war and peace. One of Peter Townsend's contributions to the latest Who album, "It's Hard," is a song entitled "I've Known No War." The song begins optimistically enough: a child of the baby boom, born after World War II, has "never been shot at or

36

gassed." But that viewpoint of being born in "victorious clover" fades to the reality of this verse:

I know I'll never know war,
And if I ever do, the glimpse will be short.
Fireball in the sky.
No front line battle cries can be heard,
And the button is pushed by a soul that's been bought.
I'll know no war.

An equally chilling image permeates the latest Pink Floyd album, "The Final Cut." The album begins with a few songs about World War II: "The Post War Dream," "The Hero's Return," and "The Gunner's Dream." Then the band faces current events in "Get Your Filthy Hands Off My Desert":

Brezhnev took Afghanistan, Begin took Beirut.
Galtieri took the Union Jack, and Maggie over lunch one day,
Took a cruiser with all hands,
Apparently to make him give it back.

The album closes with "Two Suns in the Sunset." The driver sees the sun set in the auto's rearview mirror, but "suddenly it's day again, the sun is in the East." It follows with their terrifying fantasy of the holocaust.

Like the moment when the brakes lock
And you slide towards the big truck.
You stretch the frozen moments with your fear.
And you'll never hear their voices,
And you'll never see their faces.
You have no recourse to the law anymore.
And as the windshield melts, my tears evaporate,
Leaving only charcoal to defend.
Finally I understand the feelings of the few.
Ashes and diamonds.
Foe and friend.
We are all equal in the end.

The new music doesn't always deal with war and peace exclusively in a song. Many of these songs feature a passing reference to the war games viewed on TV newscasts, or the fear of global annihilation, as if it's always in the back of one's mind, gnawing away at the soul. Maybe it's the rhetoric of "limited" nuclear war, "surviving" a nuclear war, that has made what the politicians used to refer to as the "unspeakable horror" seem closer to reality. Some of these lyrics read like the telling of a nightmare. The now defunct band The Motors related those nuclear bad dreams in the song "Nightmare Zero."

Well I was standing at the corner when I heard it on the
    radio.
The newsman told the people 'four minutes to go'. . . .
Nightmare Zero hit the town.
Nightmare Zero, mushroom cloud . . .
Everybody was screamin' as we ran to the shelter zone.
I heard a man cry "Lord above, save my soul". . . .
I thought I was goin' insane.
There's only four minutes left of oxygen to my brain.

The Jam relates an equally personal account in "'A' Bomb in Wardour Street."

I'm stranded on the vortex floor.
My head's been kicked and blood's started to pour.
Through the haze I can see my girl.
Fifteen geezers got her pinned to the door.
I try to reach her but fall back on the floor.
There's an 'A' bomb in Wardour street.
It's blown up the West End,
Now it's spreading through the city.
'A' bomb in Wardour Street
It's blown up the city,
Now it's spreading through the country.

David Byrne of the Talking Heads sings in "Life During Wartime,"

This ain't no party, this ain't no disco,
This ain't no foolin' around.
No time for dancing, or lovey dovey,
I ain't got time for that now.

But there are others who view the threat of total destruction in a different light . . . a party light. The old dance-till-the-bomb-drops attitude. Prince sings in "1999":

Everybody's got a bomb.
We could all die anyday,
But before I'll let that happen,
I'll dance my life away
Cause they say 2000 zero zero party over,

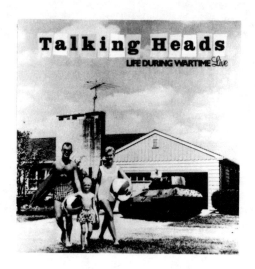

Album cover, *Life During Wartime* by The Talking Heads. Produced by The Talking Heads © Sire Recording Co, 1982, 12½" × 12½" (Terri Hemmert)

38

Oops, out of time.
So tonight I'm gonna party like it's 1999.

Tim Curry of Rocky Horror fame also chooses to dance with tongue in cheek in the seemingly lighthearted "I Do The Rock."

Carter, Begin and Sadat,
Brezhnev, Teng and Castro.
Everyday negotiate us closer to disastro.
Idi Amin and the Shah and Al Fatah is quite bizarre.
I could never get the hang of ideology.
I do the rock.

And the Ramones throw a party in "All the Way."

Doomsday, doomsday's coming, 1981
But until things blow I'm gonna have some fun.
The bubble's going to explode.
Probably never live to get old.

There is quite a bit of dark humor emerging, even from names of bands and song titles: "Holiday in Cambodia" by the Dead Kennedys, "I Love a Man In a Uniform" by the Gang of Four, and "I Never Loved Eva Braun" by the Boomtown Rats. The aforementioned Dead Kennedys come up with a unique solution to inner-city problems in "Kill the Poor."

Single about a real life version of the game "Risk" by the Spizzles © 1981 Orwell-Endwell/Chappell Music Ltd. A & M Records Ltd. (Terri Hemmert)

Efficiency and progress is ours once more,
Now that we have the Neutron bomb.
It's nice and quick and clean and gets things done.
Away with excess enemy,
But no less value to property.
No sense in war but perfect sense at home.
The sun beams down on a brand new day.
No more welfare tax to pay.
Unsightly slums gone up in flashing light.
Jobless millions wisked away.
At last we have more room to play.

And, oh yes, it's also a surefire way to lower the crime rate.

Moving from the ghetto to the suburbs, the cover of the 12-inch single of the Talking Heads' "Life During Wartime" features a what's-wrong-with-this type photo: a typical 1950s vintage family in front of their perfect suburban home, on their way to the beach—with an army tank parked in the driveway. The English Beat takes a poke at suburban patriotism in "I Am Your Flag."

So as I fly so proudly,
You will see that you won't dare break up this family.
See the happy children on parade,
With wooden guns that mother made,
And see me dancing on the breeze that blows them away.

The Dead Kennedys, in "Chemical Warfare," dream up a perverse fantasy of breaking into an arsenal to steal mustard gas and kill "a country club full of Saturday golfers."

Peace songs in the '60s were primarily concerned with the wars in Vietnam, Kent, Ohio, and Selma. The geography of peace songs in the '80s spans from Northern Ireland to Argentina, from Chile to Iran, from Poland to El Salvador, from Moscow to Washington. Songs about hand-to-hand combat with the backdrop of a mushroom cloud. The ska band Special A.K.A. takes a stand on the Middle East war in "War Crimes."

Bombs to settle arguments.
Can you hear them crying in the rubble of Beirut?
I can still see people dying.
Now who takes the blame?
The numbers are different,
The crime is still the same.
From the graves of Belsen where the innocent were burned,
To the genocide in Beirut, Israel, was nothing learned?

In "Washington Bullets," the Clash sings,

As every cell in Chile will tell,
The cry of the tortured men.
Remember Allende, and the days before,
Before the army came . . .
Please remember Victor Jara,
in the Santiago Stadium,
Es Verdas,
Those Washington bullets again.

The Clash has emerged as one of the most political bands of the decade, going as far as naming an album "Sandinista Now." Their poetic view of the Sandinistan revolution, and the way they pursue it in their art, reminds this writer of Ernest Hemmingway's attraction to the Spanish Civil War, and the way he used his art to bring that home.

In '60s anti-war songs, more often than not the U.S.A. was the villain, and L.B.J. was an easy target for protest. In the '80s, it's a

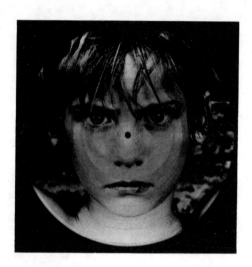

Picture disc of U2's album *War*, produced by Steve Lillywhite © Island Records Ltd, 1983, 12½″ × 12½″ (Island Records)

bit more complicated, and the U.S. now shares the heat with other nations. The Clash puts down both Washington and Moscow in "Ivan Meets G.I. Joe." They lash out at the U.S.S.R. in the song "Washington Bullets."

> If you can find an Afghan rebel that the Moscow bullets
> missed,
> Ask him what he thinks of voting communist.

And since many of the bands we've discussed here are British or Irish, there is a great deal of anti-England, anti-imperialism material. Check the Boomtown Rats, "Banana Republic" and The Clash, "London Calling" and "The Guns of Brixton." Or the English Beat, who write in the song "I Am Your Flag,"

> I ran into Northern Ireland,
> I ran into Afghanistan,
> Dying to become a man.

Of course, the soldiers and officers themselves come under fire. In the '60s, Eric Burdon of the Animals delivered his message directly to the universal soldier in "Sky Pilot." In 1981, John Cale also eliminates the middle man in "Fighter Pilot."

> Fighter pilot tell me about your life,
> And are the children well.
> Fighter pilot, what do you do with yourself at night.
> When will you ever learn.

X.T.C. is sure that Sgt. Rock will help win the battle of the sexes. Women are viewed as foreign territories waiting to be invaded. X.T.C. also predicts World War III is "drawing near" in the song "Generals and Majors." Generals and Majors are "Tired of being actionless . . . seem so unhappy 'less they have a war."

Some songs regard war as a game for overgrown boys, a game that has gone out of control. The Spizzles recorded a single called "Risk," in which a war board game becomes the real thing, and the moving of toy soldiers ultimately leads to nuclear war. The Jam (who have recorded a version of Edwin Starr's '60s Motown hit "War"), sing in "Little Boy Soldiers,"

> These days I find that I can't be bothered,
> These days I find that it's all too much,
> To pick up a gun and shoot a stranger.
> But I've got no choice so here I come.
> War games . . .

Think of honour, queen and country,
You're a blessed son of the British Empire.
God's on our side and so is Washington.

The Ramones in "Let's Go":

Don't wanna study on the G.I. Bill.
Want more action, haven't had my fill.
Mercenary, fight for anyone.
Fight for money.
Fight for fun.
Let's go . . .
Gee it's kinda scary out here.
Mosquitos are happy tonight.
Mommy, daddy, can I please come home,
Even if just for one night.
Let's go.

And you can visualize the Stranglers driving around in a tank, like an old war movie on late night TV. In "Tank" they sing,

Have you seen the bullet's high velocity.
It can blow a man's arm off at the count of three.
If I get my hands on one of those I'm something to watch out
   for.
I can drive my very own tank.
Yes I can.

Concert poster, The Clash at the Aragon Ballroom, Chicago, 1982 © Nineden Ltd, 1982 21″ × 33″ (Terri Hemmert)

There is also a whole body of work on racial wars. Some of the most significant music on this issue comes from Jamaica via Reggae records. Many of these songs deal with the violence and intolerance of racism that leads to street fighting or major battles and wars. Some of these songs evoke the same power that pumped new life into late '60s r&b charts, bringing to mind artists like Marvin Gaye and Curtis Mayfield. Tom Robinson and other English rock stars staged a campaign and series of concerts called "Rock Against Racism" in the late '70s, and that movement is remembered in Joe Jackson's, "Battleground." The Specials, one of the leading racially mixed ska bands of the ska/blue beat invasion, ask some important questions in "Why."

Do you really wanna kill me?
Tell me why, tell me why, tell me why.
We don't need no British Movement
Nor the Ku Klux Klan nor the National Front.
It makes me an angry man.

I just wanna live in peace.
Why can't you be the same?
Why should I live in fear?
This fussin' and fightin's insane.
With a Nazi salute and a steel cap boot . . .
You follow like sheep inna wolf clothes.

There are so many who have contributed to this important body of popular/political culture. Artists like the Police, Elvis Costello, Laurie Anderson and others have written and performed anti-war songs that have received commercial and critical recognition. Popular music has never pretended to offer solutions to complicated social problems but, by drawing attention to these issues, it has a purpose. Music can reflect the times, verbalize the hopes and fears of many, and create anthems for the times. Music can excite and inspire. Music has vision. Patti Smith, in her liner notes for the song "Till Victory," writes,

The lamp throws shadows across the face of a screen. Here is the image of Jean Luc Goddard offering up the celluloid strip as a materialization of the conscience of the last generation of military war. Future images flicker. The death of the machine gun. The birth and ascension of the electric guitar.

Music has a unique healing potential. Even in dealing with the most depressing of subjects—try nuclear holocaust for one—music can find a ray of hope and communicate that through head, heart and soul. It can, at its best, be a political and spiritual call to action.

In 1972, John Lennon and Yoko Ono wrote in "Sunday Bloody Sunday,"

Well it was Sunday bloody Sunday
Where they shot the people there.
The cries of thirteen martyrs filled the free Derry air.
Is there any one amongst you
Dare to blame it on the kids?
Not a soldier boy was bleeding
When they nailed the coffin lids.

Eleven years later the killing continues. Eleven years later the Irish band U2 writes in *their* "Sunday Bloody Sunday,"

I can't believe the news today.
I can't close my eyes and make it go away.
How long, how long must we sing this song?
How long?

43

How long indeed. Until the last nuclear warhead is dismantled and the last gun is thrown into the sea, only then will these modern troubadours sing only of the peace we work for, the peace we pray for everyday. Till then it's Combat Rock, with the guitar and song lyric a powerful sword.

HARRY CHAPIN was a singer, songwriter, guitarist and activist committed to the cause of peace largely through his work to end world hunger. Chapin's efforts revolved around focusing as much attention as possible on the world hunger problem so that as many people as possible would become involved and do what they could to help. As Chapin explained in a 1975 interview with Salley Rayl:

> Anyone who says that the world doesn't change is an idiot. All but maybe fifty million Americans can have an effect on this society . . . the change in the world occurs because of the on-going effort of committed minorities—*not* because of a few powerful individuals. Look at Nixon. He was a man of limited vision, limited imagination, limited intelligence and limited re-sources. It was pure determination that got him to where he was. The fact that he had a paltry vision—well . . . the fact is that most of us are sheep, but the potential for creating change is there. The problem with the World Hunger issue is that too many of us don't know the truth and without the truth we make dumb decisions. When we found out the truth about Vietnam and about Watergate, we did okay. The genius of America is knowing the truth.

Born in December of 1942, Chapin was the second son of a drummer for the Tommy Dorsey and Woody Herman bands. As a child, he and his brothers Steve and Tom performed in various

---

Writing in this chapter by Peace Museum staff members Ruth Barrett, Kerry Cochrane and Mary Anne Wolff.

groups. Harry began playing the trumpet, and eventually chose guitar as his instrument.

Chapin's music is about everyday people and events, and his fight against hunger is the fight against a problem which affects millions of people every day. He and radio talk show host Bill Ayres founded World Hunger Year (WHY) in 1975 in order to spread information and to begin offering long-term solutions to the problem. A few of WHY's projects included the formation of food co-ops and community gardens, the delivery of meals to the aged, and the changing of school lunch programs. In the beginning, Chapin and Ayres did benefit radio shows to support WHY's efforts.

Harry Chapin also organized the Food Policy Center, a Washington D.C. office which monitors current legislation and food programs. He was a lobbyist for and was appointed to President Carter's Commission on World Hunger, and was a board member of a Long Island hunger association.

Chapin was recognized by numerous organizations for his many achievements; he won first prize at the New York and Atlanta Film Festivals for his documentary *Legendary Champions*; he received two Tony Award nominations for his musical "The Night That Made America Famous"; he was the only entertainer to be awarded the Rock Music Award's "Public Service" award for two consecutive years; the Jaycees chose him as one of the Ten Most Outstanding Men in America; he won the Humanitarian Award of the B'nai Brith.

> A lot of people say, "Who are you, Harry Chapin, to be saying all this?" What they don't understand is that we're *all* supposed to be doing this. We're all supposed to be armchair experts, actively involved. It's the whole concept that this country was established on—not to be private individuals, but public citizens.

Harry Chapin was killed in an automobile accident in 1981. Soon after his death, the Harry Chapin Memorial Fund was established so that his struggle to end world hunger could continue through the work of others.

BOB MARLEY, one of the world's best-known reggae musicians, died of cancer May 11, 1981, at the age of thirty-six. During his brief but extremely prolific career, Marley made a profound impact on music, and was one of the few reggae musicians to reach an international audience. A man of profound spiritual and political commitment, he not only worked for peace in his native Jamaica, but also became a symbol of freedom to Third World people everywhere.

In 1962, the year of Jamaica's independence from British colonial rule, distributor Chris Blackwell took tapes of Jamaican music to England for release. Bob Marley's first singles were among the songs on this tape. With the Wailers, Marley would eventually become the most powerful and creative exponent of reggae music. Their songs were distinguished by their concern for social issues, such as the condition of Jamaica's slum-dwellers and Third World countries' struggles for independent rule.

Although there is no one definition of reggae, the word was popularized by a 1968 Toots and the Maytals hit called "Do the Reggay." Reggae music is characterized by its syncopated sound, produced by the prominent use of the bass guitar and bass drum, its medium tempo, and the accentuation of the second and fourth beat. Reggae is truly a "folk" music, since it derives from the musical tradition of the slaves brought to Jamaica from Africa, which was then inflected with Cuban, French, and Spanish elements. Jamaican music has always expressed the concerns of its people: social justice, religion, work, recreation, and the desire for freedom.

Bob Marley drew enthusiastic crowds wherever he performed, but the "One Love Peace Concert" in Kingston, Jamaica was possibly his most remarkable performance. On April 22, 1978, Marley joined with sixteen other top reggae musicians in a benefit performance to commemorate the twelfth anniversary of Haile Selassie's visit to Jamaica. While the money from the concert would go to provide jobs and sanitation facilities for the poor of West Kingston's ghetto, the performance was also an attempt to defuse political tensions in Jamaica. Two youth gangs had fought for years in the name of Jamaica's rival political parties, the ruling socialist People's National Party and the opposing Jamaica Labor Party, which is capitalist. Bob Marley achieved the triumph of the evening by arranging an onstage reconciliation between both the leaders of the two gangs and the politicians representing the two parties. After delivering a passionate plea for peace, Marley brought out the two youth leaders as well as Prime Minister Michael Manley of the PNP and his opponent Edward Seaga of the JLP. In a show of unity which stunned the audience of about 30,000, they all shook hands in a public truce.

Bob Marley. Photo by Anne Elliott.

Bob Marley at "One Love" peace concert bringing together Jamaican Prime Minister Michael Manley and leader of the opposing Jamaican Labour Party Edward Seaga to shake hands in a public expression of unity. Photo by Kate Simon, April 22, 1978 (Timothy White)

Bob Marley was one of the most revered figures in the third world. Wherever he traveled in the Caribbean or Africa (and Europe, for that matter), he sparked enormous outpourings of affection and admiration. A hero of mythic proportions in his own country, where he was honored with a state funeral, Marley had been given a special citation by the United Nations in 1978 on behalf of third-world nations. . . . An inspiration for black freedom fighters the world over, he was mobbed in Nigeria, Gabon and every other African country he played in or visited.*

HOLLY NEAR says, "The 'No Nukes' movement is the most urgent issue we're faced with today. Because if we don't stop the destruction of the planet, none of us will be around to enjoy the Equal Rights Amendment, to enjoy integrated schools, or whales, or music. None of these things will matter if we blow up the planet or if we fashion a nuclear power situation where radiation seeps out into the environment and creates a cancer epidemic."

Holly Near has devoted much of her career as a singer-songwriter to addressing issues of war and peace, women's rights,

*Timothy White. "Bob Marley: The King of Reggae Finds His Zion." *Rolling Stone* June 25, 1981, pp. 26–27.

nuclear power and social justice. Nationwide, her peace songs such as "No More Genocide," "It Could Have Been Me" and "Foolish Notion" have been sung at peace rallies and marches by thousands of people. She has performed at numerous peace-related events such as Peace Sunday in California and the June 12th disarmament rally in New York City in 1982. Recent tours include her "Nuclear Free Future" tour in 1980 and her 1982 tour, "Be Disarming—Challenge the Nuclear Mentality."

Her singing career began at the age of seven, when she started performing regularly at weddings and parties in her hometown of Ukiah, California. Her parents were involved in early labor struggles and in protest against nuclear weapons. Holly grew up listening to the music of Paul Robeson, Pete Seeger, and The Weavers, and she attracted the attention of a vocal coach at a very young age. By the time she entered UCLA in 1968 to study theater, Near was on her way to a career in public performance. She performed in the Broadway cast of "Hair" and in a number of television shows.

By 1971, Near was looking for a way to integrate her art and her politics. She joined the "Free the Army" tour with Jane Fonda and Donald Sutherland, and traveled with them entertaining troops in the Philippines and Japan. The tour was designed to support the growing number of G.I.'s who were resisting the war.

Soon after the "Free the Army" tour, Near became a part of the Indochina Peace Campaign, touring across the United States with Jane Fonda and Tom Hayden. The objectives of the Indochina Peace Campaign were to create a greater consciousness of the continuing war, to find a base to influence elected officials, and to find additional support for anti-war efforts.

Despite her popularity as a songwriter and singer, Near could not get a record contract to her liking; her songs were considered "too political" and her voice was "not submissive enough." As a result, Near formed her own record company, Redwood Records. She expected to sell only one or two thousand copies of the first album produced on the label (*Hang in There*), but more than 40,000 were sold.

PHIL OCHS was one of the '60s best-known musicians, whose social conscience was the powerful force behind his satirical protest songs. He was an integral part of protest gatherings for years, from Carnegie Hall concerts to Greenwich Village coffeehouses, in international folk festivals, and in marches throughout the United

Holly Near with Ronnie Gilbert of The Weavers during their 1983 tour. (Holly Near)

Original manuscript, typed and handwritten, "No More Genocide." Words and music by Holly Near, 1982, 8½" × 11" (Holly Near and Redwood Records)

Songbook, *The War Is Over*, by Phil Ochs ©
Barricade Music, Inc., 1968, 9″ × 12″ (The Old
Town School of Folk Music, Chicago)

States. Ochs was born in 1941 in El Paso, Texas, and attended a
military high school, where he belonged to the marching band. At
Ohio State University, however, he became interested in folk
music when his roommate introduced him to the songs of Pete
Seeger and Woody Guthrie. The Civil Rights and anti-war movements were also important to Ochs, and he began to write songs
which echoed his activism. He dropped out of school and moved to
New York about a year after Bob Dylan's arrival there. Dylan was
both his idol and his rival, but when Dylan turned away from
topical songs in 1964, Ochs became the acknowledged leader of this
genre among young activists.

Phil Ochs recorded six albums between 1964 and 1970. By the
late '60s, however, interest in protest songs were decreasing. Ochs
became a more radical activist, and his songs reflected this mili-
tancy. But the young people who had formerly been his audience
were turning toward the newer "electric" sound of Dylan and the
Beatles, and Ochs' following continued to wane. Although he
never recorded again after 1970, Ochs continued to participate in
the anti-war movement, organizing the May 11, 1975 "War Is
Over" rally in Central Park, which drew some 50,000 people. He
became increasingly despondent and unable to write, however, and
on April 9, 1976, he took his own life.

Poster, "The War Is Over!" Central Park, May
11, 1975, 23″ × 29″ (Don Luce)

50

Most of Phil Ochs' songs are characterized by a biting sense of satire, but he also wrote moving ballads such as "Crucifixion." Among his best-known works are "Draft Dodger Rag," "I Ain't Marching Any More," and "Outside of a Small Circle of Friends."

MALVINA REYNOLDS was a singer, songwriter and political activist whose work reflected her passionate concern for social issues. Many of her songs focused on the theme of world peace, songs such as "What Have They Done to the Rain?", "Ring Like A Bell," and "From Way Up Here."

Reynolds was born in 1900 and began her songwriting career in the fifties when the poems she had always written "began coming out with tunes attached." She composed hundreds of songs, many of which were recorded by other artists, including Harry Belafonte, Joan Baez and Pete Seeger. Reynolds herself recorded eight albums, toured internationally and at one point was a regular on Sesame Street. Her most widely known song is "Little Boxes."

Malvina Reynolds died in 1978 at the age of seventy-seven. She had written her own obituary years before because she had "made a

Original manuscript for "Way Up Here" by Malvina Reynolds © Abigail Music Co. 1962, 8½″ × 9⅜″ (Schroder Music)

51

resolution to get things done on time," and requested that on her death, contributions be sent to an organization called People Against Nuclear Power.

PAUL ROBESON, the son of a runaway slave, was a singer who became an international symbol of the artist as activist and spokesman for the oppressed. He was blacklisted and harassed for his political opinions in the '50s, but he believed in music as an agent of change, and he fought to be heard. "My weapons are peaceful," he said, "For it is only by peace that peace can be obtained. The song of Freedom must prevail."*

Robeson was born in 1898 in Princeton, New Jersey. Though his family was poor, he became a scholar, athlete, linguist, and a star of theater, film and concert stages. After he graduated from Rutgers University and Columbia Law School, he was cast by Eugene O'Neill in The Emperor Jones, where his singing voice was discovered. Robeson spent the next four years singing spirituals on tour in America.

While touring Europe before World War II, Robeson developed a hatred of fascism, and began to be considered an artist dedicated to the cause of freedom. During the Spanish Civil War he sang to troops of the International Brigade on the front lines. In 1949, after a speech at the Paris Peace Conference urging blacks to ignore the hysteria of the Cold War and to fight racism at home, President Truman forbade him to leave the U.S. Later that year, nearly one thousand reactionaries rioted at Robeson's Peekskill, New York concert in an effort to prevent his appearance. As part of a campaign to discredit his achievements, his name was removed from Who's Who in America, the All-America football rosters, and standard reference works on music and theater. After several years of blacklisting, during which his career was brought to a standstill, Robeson began to make a comeback with sellout concerts in California and New York, followed by an overseas tour. But strain and failing health forced him to retire, and he lived in seclusion from 1965 until his death in 1979, at the age of seventy-seven.

Paul Robeson was a man of tremendous personal strength and integrity. Even when he was boycotted, physically attacked, and prevented from performing in his own country, he refused to stop fighting for peace and freedom. His activism pre-dated both the

*New York Age, September 17, 1949.

Civil Rights and the anti-war movements of the '60s. In his eulogy, Bishop J. Clinton Hoggard quoted a remark Robeson had made forty years earlier: "The artist must elect to fight for freedom or slavery. I have made my choice. I have no alternative.

Paul Robeson at Paris "Peace" Parley with W.E.B. DuBois and James Crowthe, by Rene Henry, AP photo, April 22, 1949

**Musicians
on Peace**

JACKSON BROWNE

"This generation has the responsibility of deciding something for all time, and I can't think of a time in the past when that's been the case. The lives of future generations are in our hands. Jesus, it sounds pretty hokey, but it's true. I think it's been said a lot of times when it wasn't true, but it really *is* true this time."

From interview with Jane Goldman, *Rolling Stone*, October 1979

Jackson Browne. Photo by Henry Diltz
(Museum of Rock Art)

GEORGE HARRISON

"I'm always entering new phases each day as far as to just try and enjoy the moment more. Just to experience the experience deeper. That's the main thing—just to remember that we're all here now and are we all happy? And, if we're not, to try and be happier all the time, no matter what you're doing. I don't see it as this phase or that phase—the phase is to try and manifest love in your life and that's really all I can try and do."

March 1979 press conference

TOM LEHRER

"Well-wishers are constantly suggesting hilarious subject matter, such as the Vietnam War, the gradual destruction of the environ-

55

Tom Lehrer. Photograph by Don Rust.

ment, our recent presidents, etc., so that I have often felt like a resident of Pompeii who has been asked for some humorous comments on lava."

From *Too Many Songs by Tom Lehrer* (Pantheon Books, 1981)

COUNTRY JOE McDONALD

(on the Moscone Benefit)
"There's a temptation to say that because it was a big show, because it was the first and it raised a lot of money, it was a success. I don't judge things on these standards. I feel as though it's one step forward. There're about one million more things to be accomplished. This work seems to be an all-or-nothing trip."

From *Rolling Stone* article, July 8, 1982

GRAHAM NASH

"A lot of people listen to rock music, but might not think about things that are affecting humanity, so we're utilizing our own ability to reach a mass of people.

"I've always reacted to my environment. That's all I do as a writer. I get pissed off, I fall in love, I laugh, I cry, you know. I just write and react. I was doing that before Woodstock, in the Hollies, all my life. Even though twenty years have gone by, I still haven't changed my outlook on what I need to do to increase my effectiveness as a human being to help other people. A lot of people say, 'Aren't you afraid your career might take a dip?' Career? What career? Shit career. We're talking about humanity here, not one individual's career."

From a 1978 interview with Salley Rayl.

HARRY NILSSON

"We've got to shake hands and organize against violence and this [gun control] is part of it. We're killing ourselves. There may already exist enough handguns in this country to kill us all, but this whole thing is massive—that's why I talk about no difference between the little and big bullets—we'll be dead just the same. It's

A snapshot of Joe McDonald in the Navy, 1961, 2½" × 3½" (Florence McDonald)

gotta start somewhere to stop it. I told myself I'd do this for one year. It's already been two. It's like an opiate and you do, I have, gotten addicted to it. It does become an obsession because the job is never done."

From an interview with Salley Rayl during Peace Sunday, June 6, 1982

Odetta at Seva Foundation benefit, 1982.
Photograph by Lisa Law
(Museum of Rock Art)

ODETTA

"The world hasn't improved and so there is always something to sing about. I speculate there's going to be another 'folk boom'. You see, when this country gets in trouble, we listen to ourselves. And this country is in a troubled time right now with the union-buster we have in the White House."

Jet Magazine, July 1983

TOM PAXTON

"All music is effective. You wouldn't call John Lennon's 'Give Peace A Chance' a folk song, hard to call it a rock and roll song either, but it certainly played its role in the struggle against the war. All music can have an effect. It's very difficult, however, to get specific about what effect a song has . . . my job is to write the best songs I can write."

From an interview in *The Sun*

MARY TRAVERS

"There was a central question of equality in the song 'Blowin' in the Wind': 'How many years must a people exist before they're allowed to be free?' First I sang that in 1963. I sang the same song in January of this year, for political prisoners in an El Salvador prison. But now a second questions from the song applies: 'How many deaths will it take 'til he knows that too many people have died?'

"The over-all plea of the song is that there are classic inequalities of life and we must do something about them. When I sing the song I'm asking people to examine their responsibilities. Folk music does not present answers. It only articulates the questions. I

Peter, Paul and Mary.
Photograph by Paul Natkin

57

believe one person can make a difference. Collective individual consciences are powerful."

From a July, 1983 interview with Marian Christy, Chicago *Sun-Times*

BONO VOX of U2

"Revolution starts at home, in your heart, in your refusal to compromise your beliefs and your values. I'm not interested in politics like people fighting back with sticks and stones, but in the politics of love. I think there is nothing more radical than two people's loving each other, because it's so infrequent.

"I hope what's in the music comes from the hope that's in the band. I believe it's time to fight back in your spirit—right down deep inside. There is a great faith in this group."

From interview with James Henke, *Rolling Stone* June 1983

STEVIE WONDER

"We are the ones who are responsible. And we have to rid ourselves of the barriers that for the most part do not exist in the world of song. We have to make that go over into all the other different levels and place the responsibility of life on ourselves."

From an interview on Peace Sunday (June 6, 1982) with Salley Rayl

PETER YARROW

"It is not our right to speak out, it is our responsibility. To the degree that I am informed—and it is my responsibility to be informed by reading, talking, and becoming a part of this democracy—I am speaking out in my art form.

"By coming together and expressing our concerns and our commitments, we can alter a governmental policy which could injure us in a massive way, an irresponsible policy that emanates from Sacramento, from Washington, and from all the state and national governments. Once again we see that people, holding hands together believing in the efficacy of grassroots political effort can touch the wheels of power and end the insanity of what I call the doomsday bullet of nuclear power."

June, 1979 press conference on Survival Sunday II

Above: This is the guitar that John Lennon played while recording the song "Give Peace a Chance." The song was recorded from John and Yoko's room in Montreal's Queen Elizabeth Hotel where the second bed-in was held in May 1969. Joining John and Yoko on vocals were Timothy and Rosemary Leary, Tommy Smothers, Rabbi Feinberg, and the Canadian chapter of the Hare Krishnas. The drawings of John and Yoko and the legends "Amsterdam—69" and "Montreal—69" were inscribed on the guitar by John Lennon. Gibson J 160 E, 16" × 41¼" × 5" (Yoko Ono)

Gold record, *Imagine*, John Lennon Plastic Ono Band (with the Flux Fiddlers) 1971, 21½" × 17" (Yoko Ono)

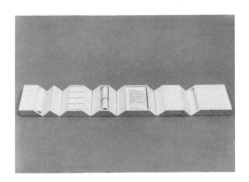

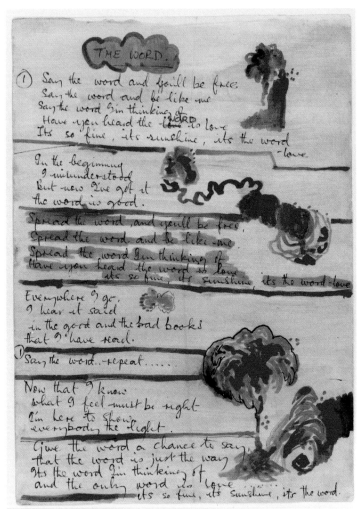

Left: Poster from the 1971 exhibit entitled "This Is Not Here" along with a conceptual art object from the exhibit, "Grapefruit Box" by Yoko Ono and John Lennon. Unfolded, the "Grapefruit Box" contains several smaller objects, including the book *Grapefruit* and a scroll covered with Ono's and Lennon's footprints. No date, 6¼″ × 7³⁄₁₆″ × 6″ (Yoko Ono)

Above: Original manuscript, "The Word," John Lennon and Paul McCartney, watercolor and ink on paper, 1965, 10″ × 14″ (Northwestern University Library)

Above: Original manuscript, handwritten on TWA flight stationary, "Death of the American" 7¼″ × 9″ (Mike Ochs)

Right: Original manuscript, with note to manager Harold Leventhal, "One Man's Hands," words by Dr. Alex Comfort, music by Pete Seeger, 1962 (Harold Leventhal)

WARRIORS OF THE SUN

By Joan C. Baez

We are the warriors of the sun
Fighting post-war battles that ~~somebody else had begun~~ *somehow never got won*
May be crazy, ~~God knows~~ (we're) young, ~~this may be~~ *This may be our final run*
We are the warriors of the sun

Tell them ~~(say)~~ we feed the hungry and we tend to the sick
Say that we're always around when the going gets thick
~~Tell~~ that we'll carry their (your) feeble and their (your) weary ones
Say we are the warriors of the sun

Black angel of Memphis is by our side
He left us precious memories just before he died
(Said) it *ain't* what you can do for me
Ah, but what can I do for thee
And the Lord came down and he set that warrior free
→ *bridge*
New York's guardian angels, you're alright
No one's gonna (will) violate granny on the subway tonight
Smiled at the child and you burried your gun
Another couple hundred warriors of the sun
Middle class collegiate types who (, they) want security
Well (the) rainbow warriors look after each others needs
Consider the lillies of the field
They reap not, neither do they sow
We're rainbow warriors of the sun and we sing as we go
bright
We see a light that's shining under Poland's skies
Organize, ~~mobilize, unite~~ but stay wise
~~You you say to~~ the momma bear, this cub's gotta run
Another couple hundred thousand warriors of the sun

Left: Original manuscript, typed and handwritten notes for "Warriors of the Sun," 8½″ × 11″ (Joan Baez, Diamonds and Rust Productions)

Above: Original manuscript, handwritten on hotel room service card, lyrics for the song, "Cambodia," 3½″ × 5⅝″ (Joan Baez, Diamonds and Rust Productions)

Above: Bob Marley memorial stamps. In 1981 Jamaica released a set of postage stamps commemorating Bob Marley. These seven stamps were reproduced from photographs taken by his wife, Rita Marley. (Doug Schimmel)

Right: Japanese "Woodstock" tickets. After the success of the Woodstock Festival, people in other countries tried to organize similar events. These are rare tickets from a proposed Japanese festival, which was never held. 1969, 2½″ × 7″ (Museum of Rock Art)

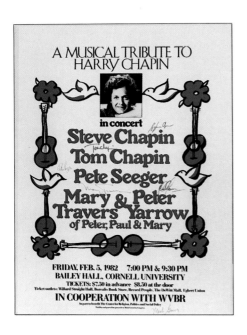

Left top: Poster of musical tribute to Harry Chapin, signed by the performers. February 5, 1982, 20″ × 25¼″ (Sandy Chapin)

Left bottom: Poster, "John Sinclair Freedom Rally," featuring speakers Rennie Davis, Allen Ginsberg, Bobby Seale, Jerry Rubin, and others, and music by John Lennon, Yoko Ono, Archie Shepp, Roswell Rudd, Phil Ochs, Commander Cody, David Peel, and others. Ann Arbor, MI., 1971, 28″ × 16″ (Mike Rivers)

Above: Poster, "From Vietnam Veterans to the World: A Night of Peace and Healing." This is the poster from a concert held to benefit the Vietnam Veterans Project, a coalition of veterans' organizations dedicated to improving the veterans' image while serving as an information clearinghouse. May 28, 1982, 21¼″ × 13¼″ (Vietnam Veterans Project)

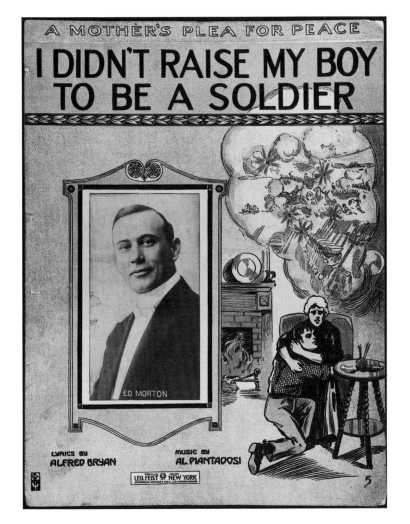

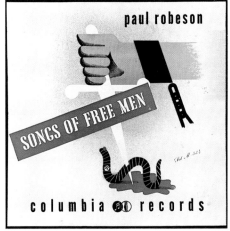

Above: Sheet music, "A Mother's Plea for Peace: I Didn't Raise My Boy to be a Soldier," Brian/Piantadosi, 1915 10½″ × 15¼″ (Anonymous gift)

Right top: Sheet music, "The Letter That Never Reached Home," Leslie/Grossman/Gottler, 1917, 10¾″ × 10½″ (University of Illinois)

Right bottom: *Songs of Free Men*, Paul Robeson. Columbia Records, Set 534, no date, 12″ × 10¾″ (Rick Steinberg)

Fourth Boise Peace Quilt. Presented to Pete Seeger in recognition of his decades of work for peace. 1983, 95″ × 95″ (Boise Peace Quilt Project)

Peace Sunday: "We Have a Dream..."

SALLEY RAYL

ON JUNE 6, 1982, 85,000 people—a mosaic of melting-pot America spanning the spectrums of age, race, religion, culture and ideology—blanketed the bleachers and the field of the Rose Bowl in Pasadena, California. Some armed themselves with placards which offered such slogans as "Hell No! We Won't Glow!," "Better Active Today Than Radioactive Tomorrow," or "One Nuclear Bomb Can Ruin Your Whole Day." Others donned tiny blue ribbons; conspicuous or subtle, the link was evident in the badges of belief. It would have been obvious even to an extraterrestrial that this mass of humanity had convened not to cheer uniformed armies of human tanks in combat over a pigskin projectile, but to focus on the outcome of a much bigger game, one of ultimate consequence, mankind's own potential Suicide Bowl.

This crowd had gathered for "a musical-cultural-spiritual celebration of peace with justice and global nuclear disarmament"— what would become a tour de force, christened Peace Sunday. The event, held on the day before the UN's Second Special Session on Disarmament, was set to kick off "Seven Days in June," a week of nationwide rallies and demonstrations on behalf of peace coinciding with the session.

The media clamored to find similarities to Woodstock, and in the process missed the most obvious one. Like Woodstock, Peace Sunday was of its time.

On June 12th, 1982, the largest demonstration for peace in the history of the United States took place at the United Nations and in New York's Central Park. Nearly one million people gathered in New York that day in support of the Second U.N. Special Session on Disarmament. Events designed to focus attention on the Special Session took place the week before in cities around the country. The largest such event was Peace Sunday.

Peace Sunday was—in no maudlin terms—a rare, even history-making, happening. With performers such as Jackson Browne, Crosby, Stills & Nash, Linda Ronstadt, Stevie Wonder, Dan Fogelberg, Donovan, Taj Mahal, Bonnie Raitt, Joe Walsh, Timothy Schmit, Jesse Colin Young, Dave Mason, Gil Scott-Heron, Stevie Nicks, Tom Petty, Camilo Sesto, Gary U.S. Bonds, Tierra and unannounced special guests like Bette Midler, Joan Baez and Bob Dylan, the day held some memorable moments, certainly worth the $12.50 ticket price. But there was more to Peace Sunday than rock'n roll.

It began as a "dream" six months before. One of the executive producers of the event, Graham Nash, whose musical laurels with the Hollies and Crosby & Stills and sometimes Young are a part of rock history, explained: "This was basically the dream of Irving Sarnoff, a volunteer organizer for the Alliance for Survival, and Reverend James Lawson, pastor of the Holman United Methodist Church and an early follower of Dr. Martin Luther King—a dream they had coming down a mountaintop in Japan." Contact was made, and, Nash recalled, "I had my part of the dream about three in the morning on January 19th—to give people a voice who never thought they had a voice."

Peace Sunday was, in fact, sponsored by a rather unique coalition—the L.A.-based Alliance for Survival and the specially-created Interfaith Committee for the Year of Shalom, which began the project and organized such religious groups as Church Women United, Southern California Ecumenical Council, Southern Christian Leadership Conference, The Gathering, Pacific Association of Reformed Rabbis, and the Spanish Speaking Apostolate of the Roman Catholic Archdiocese as co-sponsors. Nash, Lawson, and Timothy Sexton and Stephen Sulkes of the Alliance formed the Peace Sunday Executive Committee and, supported by a cast of dozens, spent more than four months planning the "dream."

"There has never been a grouping like this before," said Sulkes, "in terms of major religious groups, rock-and-rollers and people of all ages and races and cultures putting aside any differences to work together on this event."

"We decided on the Rose Bowl," continued Nash. "And that it would take rock'n roll and religion to fill it." The performers would share the Peace Sunday stage not only with such newsmak-

Salley Rayl is a freelance writer based in California. She has written for *People, Rolling Stone* and other magazines.

Original manuscript, Graham Nash's early notes on Peace Sunday, pencil and ink on notebook paper, January 19, 1982, 8″ × 11″ (Graham Nash)

ing activists as Jane Fonda, Patti Davis Reagan, Harry Nilsson (who, since the assassination of John Lennon, has been touring the country in support of handgun control), Cesar Chavez (UFW), Ron Kovic (Vietnam Veteran), Thomas Saffer (Nat'l. Assoc. for Atomic Veterans), Petra Kelly (founding member/W. Ger.'s Green Party) and John Trudell (American Indian Movement), but with such religious leaders as Rev. Lawson, Bishop James Armstrong (president/Nat'l. Council of Churches), Thelma Adair (president/ Church Women United), Rev. Jesse Jackson (founder/director, PUSH), and Rabbi Leonard Beerman (co-founder/Interfaith Center to Reverse the Arms Race), among others. If for this reason

Gary "U.S." Bonds on stage at Peace Sunday.
Photo by Lisa Law (Museum of Rock Art)

David Crosby, Stevie Wonder on stage at Peace
Sunday. Photo by Lisa Law (Museum of Rock
Art)

alone, Peace Sunday marked an historic occasion in rock's resurgent role in the peace movement.

Still, filling the Bowl seemed nothing less than a far-reaching plan. Journalists on the peace beat had long questioned just how many people turned up at rallies because of the music, rather than the cause; and considering that most of the all-star musical line-up frequented nearly every such event and that most of those "over 30" considered day-long festival-style concerts as survival marathons, it came as no real surprise that ticket sales, in the weeks prior, weren't exactly, well . . . breaking any records. But in the last five days, groundwork laid, the celebration's momentum became a kind of magnetic force field. An additional 30,000 tickets were sold (some at a discount to low income families) and celebrities began calling, offering their support.

Ed Asner, Eileen Brennan, Jeff Bridges, LeVar Burton, Michael Douglas, Mike Farrell, Carrie Fischer, Harrison Ford, Lee Grant, Joan Hackett, Howard Hesseman, Jane Kennedy, Margot Kidder, Penny Marshall, Tim Matheson, Donna Mills, Michael Ontkean, Lorna Patterson, Martin Sheen, and Robert Walden all joined the constituency on this particular day.

As Mike Farrell so aptly noted: "I don't think that you can be in the milieu—whether it's in motion pictures, television or reality—and not come to grips with some notion of what the value of human life is . . . and that we have the power to do something about it."

Timing is everything, it's said, and, in a way that no amount of organizing could have guaranteed, Peace Sunday's timing was impeccable, right down to the weather. Los Angeles had been dismally grey for weeks, but on June 6th, even the sun refused to miss the event.

At 12:45 p.m., Graham Nash, who had been standing on a platform behind the stage, caught the first, faint strains of a familiar anthem (not the one about "bombs bursting in air") emanating from the darkness of a tunnel, signaling the start of the opening ceremonies.

. . . "All we are sa-ying—is give peace a chance . . " Humming the day's theme song on kazoo, the movement's clown of renown, Wavy Gravy, emerged from the tunnel leading a procession of 2,000 children down an open path amidst the throng of people on the field. Buzzing or warbling, bobbing posters or carrying banners, faces painted with peace signs, the children with a back-to-the-garden pomp and circumstance took their winding position.

Graham Nash and his wife Susan, moments after the grand finale of Peace Sunday.
Photo by Jan Butchofsky © 1982

63

John Lennon's words, more than a decade after they were written, were revitalized through the children's voices, heartfelt and kinetic. As if on cue, the audience chimed in and the once-faint strains of "Give Peace a Chance" rang throughout the stadium.

The crowd thundered its alliance when the children, in what has become symbolic gesture, launched thousands of different colored balloons. The fervor of that opening lasted throughout the 10-hour day.

Peace Sunday's first speaker, Rev. Lawson, in a speech which harkened back to King's famous civil rights address, introduced the day's theme, saying in part: . . . "To each other we may indeed say We Have A Dream . . . we are brothers and sisters . . . we have the right to live in peace. . . ."

Despite the number of last-minute additions and its near three-hour overtime, Peace Sunday was a well-paced event, percolating from moment to moment, taking on different meanings for different people. And there were moments for everyone. Moments of musical reunion—when Joan Baez stopped midway through her set to introduce her surprise guest, Bob Dylan, much in the same way she introduced him in the early '60s, and the two duoed on "With God On My Side," an early protest song, and, the one everybody knew the words to, "Blowin' In the Wind;" and when Crosby, Stills and Nash stirred memories with "Wooden Ships," . . .

Moments of poignancy—when Michael Kennedy, on the 14th anniversary of his father's assassination at the Ambassador Hotel in Los Angeles, ended a moving speech by saying: "we are committed now, as my father was then, to the ancient dream of which he spoke so many times- 'to tame the savageness of man and make gentle the life of the world,' " . . .

of sheer entertainment—when Bette Midler in a joking reference to Woodstock, warned the crowd about the "green acid," . . .

of logic—when Nilsson told the people about the difference between the "big bullets" and the "little bullets": "There is no difference," . . .

of observation—when Bishop Armstrong reviewed the event this way: "there is a genuine awareness of what people are doing here—making a commitment to peace." . . .

of universal communication—when a fragile, grey-haired, primly dressed woman standing near the front of the stage, began to boogie as Stevie Wonder broke into "Do I Do," . . .

of entreaty—when Jane Fonda and Linda Ronstadt urged the

people to use the "power of the vote;" and when Cesar Chavez asked the crowd not to buy Dole pineapples and bananas . . .

of reflection—when Baez, backstage, mused: "Today was terrific. It will be very curious, after a day like this, to see if people move themselves into the educational situation—actually go home and do something."

And, in the end, there was a final moment of unity—when the day's musical performers joined Jackson Browne and Gary U.S. Bonds onstage and, arm in arm, ended Peace Sunday the way it began, singing with the audience, "Give Peace a Chance."

While it's still too early to adequately assess the impact of Peace Sunday, this much can be said—the performers and speakers raised

Joan Baez and Bob Dylan on stage. Photo by Henry Diltz (Muscum of Rock Art)

65

$250,000 (divided equally between the Alliance and the Interfaith Committee), and Californians used 'the power of the vote' to pass an initiative requesting that the federal government support a bilateral freeze program.

The media clamored to find similarities to Woodstock, and in the process missed the most obvious one. Like Woodstock, Peace Sunday was of its time. It was in the stars, and, fueled perhaps by the same brand of togetherness, it . . . just happened. In hindsight, Peace Sunday may come to be regarded as rock's next 'small step' for mankind.

As the last of the performers left the stage, one lifetime member of the Woodstock Nation pondered aloud to a friend, "And people still ask whatever happened to the revolution." The friend chuckled and responded, "Yeah, we know. Don't we? It just took a long lunch."

For Dr. King:
A Holiday

STEVIE WONDER

JANUARY 15, 1981—At least 175,000 people were assembled on that now historic day. It was the day we marched in Washington, D.C., at the Washington Monument to respectfully demand that the United States Congress declare the birthday of Dr. Martin Luther King Jr. a national holiday. There were millions of other Americans as one with me—physically, mentally, and spiritually—as we gathered to let the world know that we protested the killing of great leaders. It is amazing that a man who received the Nobel Peace Prize is not duly recognized for his contributions that liberated not only minorities but all people: white, Black, red, yellow and brown. Our nation's inability to honor Dr. King with a national holiday echoes the very ills of the society he refuted.

The fight for peace in this country is not being waged to help only one group of people. The quest for peace is meant to benefit us all. We must reflect on its meaning and necessity; if we don't, it will mean devastation, a devastation that will encompass all people, all races, all colors. Dr. King cared about all of us, about seeing that *all* Americans benefit from what was promised to us in the Constitution over 200 years ago. Certainly, America can be proud of a man who represented the great principles, the great teachings of the heroic messengers of mankind down through the ages, teachers who delivered the message of peace, brotherhood, love, basic human dignity and freedom.

The quest for peace is meant to benefit us all.

Reprinted by permission from *Essence* magazine, where this article appeared in January, 1982.

Stevie Wonder with coordinators of the MLK National Holiday project announcing plans for the second march on Washington, D.C., November, 1981, Los Angeles Press Club (Black Bull Music)

Ours is a universe of rhythm, a melody of movement, a symphony of light, heat and sound—a musical universe of time in space. We exist in a universe of vibrations requiring, for peace and harmony, that all systems be in tune and in touch. The spiritual legacy of Dr. King still inspires us. We came to Washington D.C., not only to show this nation that it should recognize what he achieved; we gathered to remind ourselves that the road that still has to be traveled is no less rough than it was centuries or decades ago. The obstacles across our path have grown, especially with our administration's current economic policies. The administration's attitude toward the have-nots, its position of pushing the Dr. King bill farther down on its list of priorities, exemplifies how we must make an even louder noise for what we want. Those who legislate our future must admit that in 1982, America still has a race problem—the administration and the legislators must hear us.

There are significant and prevalent concerns occupying my mind as well as the minds of others. There is a growing desire for all Americans to search for something positive in which to believe. The only way that we can look forward to the positive is to hold on and believe in the positive forces given to us from the past. Dr. King shows us the positive. Here is a man who gave not only his energy, his soul, his sensitive heart, but his life. He looked beyond all cultural, color and racial boundaries to see a better tomorrow. His life was dedicated to working for civil and economic rights for all people. He gave to Americans what all leaders of this potentially great nation should give. That is why a spiritual King never dies.

It has been said that the good guys always win. That did not prove so in the case of Dr. King. Yet he was not just a good guy. He was a man among men, a living manifestation of the modern people's king of peace. He is forever prevalent in the minds, in the hearts, and on the lips of all people because we know that we will overcome.

You may ask why Stevie Wonder is involved in the quest to make Dr. King's birthday a national holiday. I am not only Stevie Wonder the artist and performer; I am a man and a citizen of this nation. I feel that as an artist, my responsibility is to communicate messages that improve the lives of us all.

Poster promoting Martin Luther King National Holiday March sponsored by Stevie Wonder, January 1982. Artwork by Avery Clayton, 1970, 17″ × 22″ (Black Bull Music)

How *Waist Deep in the Big Muddy* Finally Got on Network Television in 1968

PETE SEEGER

MOST OF MY LIFE I have assumed that the kind of songs I sing would not normally get played on the airwaves. I pointed to examples like Woody Guthrie's song, "This Land Is Your Land" to show that they don't *have* to get played on the airwaves. If it's a real good song, it will get spread around anyway.

But in 1967 I wrote what I thought was a real good song, and I knew there wasn't time for it to get around the country. People were being killed every day in Vietnam. I had a recording contract with Columbia Records at that time, and my friends there even agreed to put out a record of it; but the sales department just laughed at us both. The records stayed on the shelves and weren't even sent to the stores.

But two young comedians had a successful television show, and they asked their bosses if I could be a guest on their show. The Smothers Brothers were turned down by CBS TV at first, but finally they said O.K. I flew out to California and sang some songs that had been sung by American soldiers in four different wars— the American Revolution, the Civil War, World War I, and lastly this song, "Waist Deep in the Big Muddy." It was a story song, kind of an allegory, describing a bunch of soldiers training during World War II and the captain tells them to ford a muddy river. But as it gets deeper the sergeant urges they turn around. The Captain says, "Don't be a Nervous Nelly. Follow me." But the Captain is drowned and they find his body stuck in the old quicksand. And the last verse says, "Every time I read the paper, those old feelings

Of course, a song is not a speech, you know.

71

Pete Seeger. Photo by Lisa Law (Museum of Rock Art)

come on/We are waist deep in the Big Muddy and the big fool says to push on."

Son of a gun, when the show was supposed to be played on the air, the song had been scissored out of the tape by the higher-ups at CBS Television. Now the Smothers Brothers did a clever thing. They took their argument to the newspapers and they got lots of free publicity. They said, "CBS censors our best jokes, they censored Seeger's best song. It ain't fair." Finally in the month of January, 1968, the word came from New York, "O.K., O.K., you can sing the song if you want."

72

On 48 hours' notice I flew out to California, taped the song, and this time 7 million people saw it and even got some extra newspaper publicity. Only one station, I think, in Detroit, scissored the last verse out of the tape.

Did the song do any good? No one can prove a damned thing. It took tens of millions of people speaking out, before the Vietnam War was over. A defeat for the Pentagon, but a victory for the American people.

Of course, a song is not a speech, you know. It reflects new meanings as one's life's experiences shine new light upon it. (This song does not mention Vietnam or President Johnson by name.) Often a song will reappear several different times in history or in one's life as there seems to be an appropriate time for it. Who knows. Here are the complete words of the song (I'm supposed to tell people that it's copyright 1967 by T.R.O.):

It was back in 1941.
I was a member of a good platoon.
We were on maneuvers in Lou'siana one night by the light of
   the moon.
The Captain told us to ford a river.
That's how it all begun.
We were knee deep in the Big Muddy,
And the big fool said to push on.

The Sergeant said, "Sir, are you sure this is the best way back
   to the base?"
"Sergeant Gowan, I've forded this river
About a mile above this place.
It'll be a little soggy, but just keep sloggin'.
We'll soon be on dry ground."
We were waist deep in the Big Muddy,
And the big fool said to push on.

The Sergeant said, "Sir, with all this equipment, no man will
   be able to swim."
"Sergeant, don't be a Nervous Nelly,"
The Captain said to him.
"All we need is a little determination.
Men, follow me. I'll lead on."
We were neck deep in the Big Muddy,
And the big fool said to push on.

All at once the moon clouded over.
We heard a gurglin' cry.

A few seconds later the Captain's helmet
Was all that floated by.
The Sergeant said, "Turn around, men.
I'm in charge from now on."
And we just made it out of the Big Muddy
With the Captain dead and gone.

We stripped and dived and found his body
Stuck in the old quicksand.
I guess he didn't know that the water was deeper
Then the place he'd once before been.
Another stream had joined the Big Muddy
About a half mile from where we'd gone.
We were lucky to escape from the Big Muddy
When the big fool said to push on.

Now I'm not going to point any moral—
I'll leave that for yourself.
Maybe you're still walking, you're still talking,
You'd like to keep your health.
But every time I read the papers, that old feeling comes on,
We're waist deep in the Big Muddy
And the big fool says to push on.

Waist deep in the Big Muddy,
The big fool says to push on.
Waist deep in the Big Muddy,
The big fool says to push on.
Waist deep, neck deep, soon even a tall man will be over his
    head.
We're waist deep in the Big Muddy,
And the big fool says to push on.

Sorry for all the mistakes in typing

Pete Seeger

May, 1983

74

Dear Anthony

JOAN BAEZ

DEAR ANTHONY and members of Perspective—

I'm happy to write you a few words on the subject of peace.

Let me begin by throwing you a curve. Although I use the word "peace" occasionally in speeches and songs, it is not a word I like very much. It's used for anything from an excuse for spending two hundred and some billion dollars on weapons, to a cosmic and mushy state that can be reached by kissing the feet of a guru (and paying him enough money). More generally it seems to represent a static condition that we can reach some day, no matter how befuddled we are as we go looking for it. Aldous Huxley, a great English author, said: "Everyone wants peace, but few people want to do the things which make for peace."

The term I would use in its place is "nonviolence," and I'd try to always link it with action—nonviolent action—nonviolent change—nonviolent revolution. Because in order to get peaceful ends, we must be both nonviolent and very active. In order to have a world without war and exploitation, we must stop killing (no matter what grand excuse we are using) and exploiting other people. Just to take that stand—to disarm yourself and become engaged in action at the same time is a lot of work. To organize that on even a small scale is a lifetime (or two) of work!

The letter above was written by Joan Baez for an issue of *Perspective*, a school paper put out by students at East Meadow High School in East Meadow, New York.

Joan Baez (Photo by Paul Natkin)

I'm delighted to be able to refer you to Richard Attenborough's new movie, *Gandhi*. If you haven't seen it yet, please go one evening. It finally explains to the public in an exciting and moving way, the origins, not of nonviolence so much as its use as a mass movement against oppression. Gandhi knew that in order to *get* peace we had to *do* peace, and that's what his entire life was about—well portrayed in the film. To *do* nonviolence is not passive or in any way easy. I have been a fighter all my life, and am proud to call myself, like Gandhi, a nonviolent soldier.

Nonviolence as an organized way to social change, then, is very new—so it is little known, much misunderstood and misinterpreted, and, when properly understood, a scary prospect. But it's worth looking into, and, I'm convinced, is the only realistic tool we have at our disposal which can really bring about a world in which peace means more than the absence of war—although the mere *concept* of eliminating war is enough for a start, wouldn't you say?

The very best to all of you,
love,

Joan Baez
Jan. 20, 1983

They All Sang Songs of Peace: Pacifism and Folk Music in the 1960s

JEROME RODNITZKY

MELANIE'S 1970 HIT SONG, "Candles in the Rain," was based on her experiences in a candlelight peace protest against the Vietnam War. Most listeners were unaware of the song's origins, but by 1970 so many folk-oriented popular songs had vaguely pacifist phrases that origins were irrelevant. Melanie's song talked about the young people she observed in the candlelight protest, but it could have applied to an entire generation. "We bled inside each others wounds," she sang. "We all had caught the same disease," she continued. "We all sang the songs of peace," she concluded. Indeed, Melanie's generation was ready for songs of peace.

The generation of the 1960s had grown up entirely in wartime—either the cold war of the Korean era or the hot war of Vietnam. They were the first generation to observe daily combat on television. Added to this was the smaller-scale, yet more personal, violence of political assassinations and the periodic outbursts of rioting in the racially-torn inner city ghettoes. If ever a generation had good cause to reject violence, it was the shell-shocked youth of the sixties. The untimely death of President Kennedy in 1963 offered the first jolt. As songwriter Phil Ochs noted in "That Was The President," his memorial ballad for John Kennedy, for a person "so filled with life even death was caught off guard."

However, the deaths of John Kennedy, Martin Luther King, Jr., Malcolm X, and Robert Kennedy—all cut down in their prime

Never before in history had music meant so much to a generation.

Jerome Rodnitzky teaches history at the University of Texas at Arlington and is the author of *Minstrels of the Dawn*, a history of folk music.

Joan Baez and Martin Luther King marching in
Grenada, Mississippi, 1966 (Joan Baez and
Diamonds and Rust Productions)

with little apparent reason—deeply impressed young Americans
with the capriciousness, flimsiness and tragedy of life. Moreover,
as the Vietnam casualties (from young American troops to infant
Vietnamese) continued to pile up in America's most disgusting, ill-
conceived and unproductive war, the tragedy of dying young and
violently was further embedded in the collective consciousness.
Almost everyone knew at least one young American struck down

in the complicated civil war thousands of miles from our shores. Meanwhile, at home, violence continued to escalate on city streets and, after 1965, to appear even on prestigious college campuses like Berkeley and Columbia.

The years 1965 and 1966 were turning points for pacifism during the decade. Martin Luther King, Jr., had solidly identified the civil rights movement with nonviolence, although it later became clear that the movement's nonviolence was tactical rather than philosophical. Also, the early "New Left" and anti-Vietnam movements, especially active during the 1964 presidential campaign and the first year of the Johnson administration, were clearly pacifist in mood. However, after 1965 the Black movement increasingly moved toward Malcolm X's doctrine of counter-violence, and the campus-based New Left steadily moved toward their own inconsistent position of anti-militarism at home, coupled with a call for revolutionary guerilla warfare in the developing countries. Folksinger Joan Baez, a self-proclaimed pacifist, told a Berkeley crowd of 1,000 undergraduates that she was about to lead a march into the administration building: "Have love as you do this thing and it will succeed."

However, Baez quickly wrote off the Free Speech Movement as an "unviolent" movement (ready to switch to violence to obtain its goals) as opposed to a truly nonviolent movement. Baez, who described herself as a "nonviolent soldier," once jokingly warned a crowd of protestors: "Be nonviolent or I'll kill you." Baez's comment was surely innocent, but beneath contemporary nonviolent activism there existed the seeds of violence.

The popular music of the 1960s faithfully traced the rising youthful tides of both idealistic pacifism and frustrated, impatient violence, while suggesting the close relationships between the two. Never before in history had music meant so much to a generation. The new music and the records that disseminated it became the real alternate media as opposed to the underground press. If there was a counterculture, surely it lived between the microgrooves. As rock performer Frank Zappa had noted, many American youths were not loyal to flag, country or doctrine, but only to music. Thus, one cannot really study any aspect of the youth culture without considering its popular music.

In the hyper-emotional pacifist songs of the sixties, the lyrics were usually double-edged and mirrored the ambivalent view of nonviolence common to the era's youthful activists. The songs spoke eloquently for nonviolence, but they often warned of "the

Assorted sheet music: songs of antiwar sentiment during the Vietnam War (Carl Fischer Music)

79

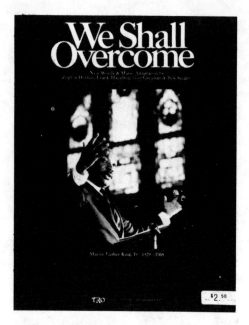

Sheet music, "We Shall Overcome," new words and arrangements by Zilphia Horton, Frank Hamilton, Guy Carawan, and Pete Seeger, © Ludlow Music Inc, 1969, 9½″ × 11″ (Carl Fischer Music)

Manuscript, "We Shall Overcome," by Horton, Hamilton, Carawan, and Seeger, 1960, 9½″ × 12½″ (Harold Leventhal)

fire next time." The lyrics were filled with images of hell-fire and brimstone. Behind the New Testament gentleness was a violent Old Testament sternness. Yet, the inconsistent treatment of violence in folk-protest music had a long history. American protest songs had always been fascinated with violent subject matter. The labor songs of twentieth-century unions such as the militant Industrial Workers of the World before World War One and the industry-wide unions of the 1930s (like the United Mineworkers) commonly described both the violence of company thugs and the necessity of worker resistance. Thus, one verse of IWW writer Joe Hill's ballad, "There Is Power In The Union," noted: "If you've had 'nuff of the blood of the lamb/Then join in the grand industrial band," and "If you like sluggers to beat off your head/Then don't organize and all unions despise." Likewise, Woody Guthrie, the father of recent folk-protest, wrote in the 1930s about a "Union Maid" who did not fear "goons or ginks or company finks," but would stick to the union despite physical threats. Indeed, Guthrie's proletarian hero was the fictional Tom Joad from Steinbeck's *The Grapes of Wrath*, who met violence with physical resistance.

Not surprisingly, during World War Two Guthrie inscribed on his guitar: "This machine kills fascists." Folksinger Pete Seeger, the future leader of the protest song movement, later adopted a more peaceful message. In the 1960s Seeger wrote on his banjo: "This machine surrounds hate and forces it to surrender." However, during World War Two, it was Seeger who enlisted in the Army while Guthrie joined the Merchant Marine.

The folk ambivalence toward war was complicated by an underlying belief that wars were largely fought for the benefit of wealthy capitalists and that war was the health of the capitalist economy. For example, in 1948 Irwin Silber, a folk-protest editor, recalled a song parody written in the thirties about World War I to the tune of "I Want a Girl Just Like the Girl That Married Dear Old Dad!"

I want a war,
Just like the war
That made my daddy rich.

It was a war
And the only war
For daddy that son of a ---
Wall Street banker.

A good old-fashioned war,
Red, white and blue.

Just the kind of war
For me and you.

Oh, I want a war,
Just like the war
That made my daddy rich.

However, in the late 1950s and early 1960s, with Korea still a bitter memory, protest singers turned their attention to the domestic scene and embraced pacifism more wholeheartedly. As usual, Pete Seeger's activities illustrated the trend.

Seeger, like most protest singers, identified with pacifism largely because of his involvement with the early Southern civil rights movement. Along with Guy Carawan, Seeger had taken an old Baptist hymn, developed at the Highlander Folk School in Manteagle, Tennessee, and further refined it into its present form. We know this organizing song as "We Shall Overcome," the anthem of the civil rights movement. Fittingly, the copyright and royalties to the ballad were generously assigned to the Student Non-violent Coordinating Committee; and, although they soon changed the second word in their name to National (while also changing their nonviolent stance), they still owned the song.

Throughout the sixties, Seeger projected a pacifist image in his songs and action. At the start of the decade, the Kingston Trio's version of Seeger's frankly pacifist song about the futility of war, "Where Have All the Flowers Gone?," was a smash hit in America and in translated form the ballad swept Europe as well.

Likewise, "The Hammer Song," which Pete wrote with Lee Hays, was made into a hit by the popular folk trio Peter, Paul, and Mary. The ballad was largely a civil rights song, but the chorus keyed on a phrase about love between brothers "all over this land," and the tone was clearly pacifist. The song urged people to sing about freedom, justice, and love rather than to fight for goals. It was not until 1964 that Malcolm X suggested that singing "We Shall Overcome" would not bring change and that true freedom fighters were too busy fighting to sing. Meanwhile, Seeger and most other protest singers sang and wrote about peace. At their concerts they often sing Ed McCurdy's song, "Last Night I Had the Strangest Dream," which depicted a worldwide peace treaty that ended war forever. And even nursery rhymes were bent to the needs of peace. Maurice Sugar's song, "Modern Mother Goose," noted:

Old Mother Hubbard slammed the door of her cupboard

Sheet music for Pete Seeger's "Where Have All the Flowers Gone?" which was translated into many foreign languages © 1961, 9½″ × 11″ (Harold Leventhal)

Yoko Ono's single "Now or Never" incorporates a famous photograph of the My Lai massacre © Apple Records, 1972, 7″ × 7⅛″ (Yoko Ono)

81

And then went out marching for peace,
She knew that the whistle of rocket and missile
Would mean that all eating would cease.

The development of Seeger's own lyrics provide a good example of how Vietnam blurred the distinction between those who hated violence and those who particularly hated the violence of American intervention in Asia. His anti-war song, "Bring Them Home," argued on the one hand that those who were fighting did not have the right weapons, since the real enemies were "hunger and ignorance," and that what the world needed was "teachers, books, and schools." Yet, in another verse Seeger says that he is not "really a pacifist," because, if his country were invaded he could be found "out on the firing line."

The few pacifist songs which were widely played on commercial stations were received in a politically mixed climate. In 1965, while the Vietnam War was escalating, Buffy Saint-Marie wrote her vehemently pacifist ballad, "Universal Soldier." Although the song was a runaway success, Glen Campbell, who recorded the hit single, supported the war and was quoted as saying that "anyone who wouldn't fight for his country was no real man." And, later that year, the California-based rock duo of Jan and Dean parodied "Universal Soldier" in a song entitled "Universal Coward," the story of a man "who ran from Uncle Sam," "ran from Vietnam," and never read "the writing on the wall."

Yet singing protest marchers continued to reflect a communal pacifist spirit manifested in such loose slogans as "make love, not war," and such romantic events as torchlight parades for peace. Thus, in 1969 a University of Wisconsin student criticized *Newsweek* magazine for concentrating on the few violent incidents in a campus demonstration while ignoring "the 10,000 peaceful marchers singing together by torchlight."

Whether by torchlight or by daylight, there was magic in mass singing. Perhaps the charisma came through best in the key line of the Paul McCartney-John Lennon song, *"The Word"*: "Say the word and be like me. Say the word and you'll be free." The word was, of course, love, but at a given rally the magic word more likely became peace. In this atmosphere rock writers began routinely inserting pacifist sentiments in their songs, and since all could agree that peace was generally desirable, peace lost its meaning whenever it was taken out of a specific context.

Yet, a few writers managed to confront the issues of peace and

Single produced by Entertainment Industry for Peace and Justice, cover design by Jane Fonda, recorded in San Francisco, July, 1971, 7½″ × 10⅜″ (Country Joe McDonald)

violence directly. By 1965 Bob Dylan had ceased writing songs against anything, but he had already penned some admirable anti-war lyrics in "Masters of War," "A Hard Rain's A-Gonna Fall," and especially in his most artful protest song, "With God on Our Side." However in a 1964 song, titled "My Back Pages," Dylan declared that he had been much older when writing these political protests and that he was "younger than that now." Instead of writing about doves in the white sea sand, he now wrote about black motorcycle madonnas. Taking over his throne as the leading protest singers were Phil Ochs, Tom Paxton and Joan Baez, and ever present was Pete Seeger, the keeper of the folk-protest flame.

Baez and Paxton were rather consistently pacifist, but Phil Ochs, much more in tune with the increasingly frustrated youth, showed more ambivalence toward pacifism. As the Vietnam War intensified from 1965 to 1967, Ochs became more cynical in view and more militant in verse. Back in 1965, Ochs' "I Ain't Marching Anymore" album had been frankly pacifist. Ochs had summed it up in the title song when he told the listener to "call it peace" or "treason, call it love or call it reason," but he was not "marching anymore." On the liner notes, Ochs described the title song as hovering between "pacifism and treason, combining the best qualities of both." In another song from the album, called "Draft Dodger Rag," Ochs told an army sergeant that if he ever found a war "without blood and gore" then he would "be the first to go." And, elsewhere, in the song "Links on the Chain," Ochs' message was that the violent union struggles had taught his generation of protestors that "you gotta fight, you gotta strike, to get what you are owed."

In his last serious album, "Rehearsals for Retirement," which appeared in 1969, Ochs attacked the paranoia of the police in a song called, "I Kill Therefore I Am," and the violent inclinations of rightist groups in "Pretty Smart on My Part," but he did not completely endorse nonviolence. Rather, in "A New Age," Ochs indicated that the younger generation, who had learned the lessons of violence, was leading society towards an upheaval and subsequent rebirth. The chorus of "A New Age" noted that whereas "soldiers had their sorrow" and "the wretched had their rage," we should "pray for the aged," since it was the "dawn of another age."

The hazy pacifist images of some songs mirrored the sometimes superficial pacifism displayed at anti-War rallies after 1968. The huge crowds at these rallies certainly encouraged and exuded a peaceful togetherness. For example, in late 1969 a crowd of 8,000

Sing Out Magazine, October-November 1962, cover photograph of Bob Dylan by John Cohen © Sing Out Inc, 1962, 5½" × 8½" (Sing Out Magazine)

Album cover, *I Ain't Marching Any More*, by Phil Ochs © Elektra Records, 1965, 12½" × 12½" (Michael Ochs)

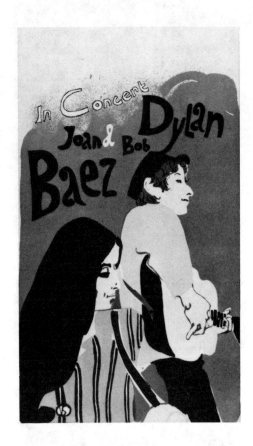

Rare handbill from Dylan and Baez concert in the early '60s, 5½″ × 9½″ (Manny Greenhill)

Stanford University students met for an evening of anti-War speeches and appropriate folk-and-rock music, and afterward one student reported: "There was a feeling of brotherhood there. I don't know how I'll feel tomorrow, but I belong tonight." However, a 1967 student-led march for peace at the Pentagon symbolized the confusion of mass peace rallies. A cheerleader led the crowd in cheers for peace and the dialogue went as follows:

> Cheerleader: What do we want?
>
> Crowd: Peace!
>
> Cheerleader: When?
>
> Crowd: Now!
>
> Cheerleader: Why?
>
> Crowd: (Dead silence, followed by a shrill female voice) Because.

Yet peace was clearly more commercially acceptable after 1968. For example, John Lennon's instant 1969 peace anthem, "Give Peace a Chance," was written during four well-publicized days in bed with his wife, Yoko Ono, in a suite in Montreal's Queen Elizabeth Hotel. According to Lennon, peace had "to be sold to the man in the street," and thus John wanted "to make peace big business for everybody." Evidently Lennon succeeded, for "Give Peace a Chance" sold 900,000 copies in the U.S. and another 400,000 world-wide.

It is still too early to assess what effect pacifist songs had on this generation above and beyond the negative attitudes toward war and violence generated by the 1960's. In any case, for the most serious pacifist singers and writers the victory was clearly in the struggle. For example, referring to her fellow advocates of nonviolence and their lack of success at converting American society, Joan Baez noted: "We're really a flop," but she quickly added: "Only violence is a bigger flop."

The Art of the Concert Poster and the Album Cover

PAUL S. CARUSO

PABLO PICASSO, Aubrey Beardsley and Henri de Toulouse Lautrec were all poster artists, elevating ads to fine art. World War I became the first "poster war." James Montgomery Flagg's "Uncle Sam" posters and other brightly colored lithographs promoting war bonds became the forerunners of today's poster evolution.

Posters have always reflected social change, revolution and peace, especially in their promotion of other art forms: music, theatre and illustration itself.

Jazz art of the 1920s gave way to stately Deco just as music entered the Big Band era. The cool industrial pastel art of the 50s was likewise shattered by the chaotic colors and forms of Pop and Psychedelic art which paralleled the growth of Rock & Roll.

By the late 1960s, rock musicians demanded artistic control of album covers and posters. In San Francisco, the Fillmore and Avalon Ballrooms gave a new breed of poster artists complete freedom to develop extraordinary concepts in contemporary illustration.

These poster artists were liberated from the rules and restrictions of advertising. They pushed themselves to their limits and returned with new visions and passions. Their use of the 60s symbols became incorporated in their illustrations. As they introduced the "hippies" to their new music, their art became the symbols of the peace movement. The "street people" now banded together to

The combination of artist and musician is still active in today's movement.

Paul S. Caruso is the founder and director of the Museum of Rock Art, Hollywood, California.

85

Concert poster from one of the Fillmore
Concerts, 1967 © Bill Graham, 1967, 14″ × 24″

show their power, consciousness and disagreement with nuclear war.

Through the talents of Stanley Mouse, Bob Fried, Rick Griffin, Bob Seidemann and others, posters once again demanded cultural revolution as the Woodstock generation evolved new art forms. Like the music they served, these posters have become an important historical reference to the growth of peace fueled by the music of Rock & Roll.

As the peace movement grew, rock musicians banded together and created specific music to show their distrust with world politics. The combination of artist and musician is still active in today's movement for total nuclear disarmament and World Peace.

Origins and Inspirations of the Protest Song

R. SERGE DENISOFF

MUSIC HAS TRADITIONALLY been a medium for popular thought, and the peace movement, from its inception, has used music to communicate its message. In the last few decades the anti-war movement has been promoted by men and women who have had not only the commitment to social change, but the means of broadcasting their thoughts through the mass media. This access to a wider audience has allowed the acceptance of peace music recorded by popular musicians as "pop" music, sometimes even before the peace message itself is understood. As a result, many anti-war songs of the sixties and seventies have been adopted as anthems of the peace movement while also being recognized as good music in their own right. The attention given to peace music and musicians has increased public interest in the origins and inspirations of the protest song.

American leftists originally stumbled upon the folk-styled protest song in the hamlets of the rural South, where folk songs frequently addressed every phase of life and experience. The most proletarian of all the American leftist movements, the Industrial Workers of the World (known as the Wobblies), who used songs extensively, primarily adapted the songs of the streets and the

Although the issues and the songs change, the power of music to bring people together in the expression of their opinions has never been diminished.

Portions of this article appeared in *Great Day Coming: Folk Music and the American Left* (Urbana-Champaign: University of Illinois Press, 1977) and *Sing a Song of Social Significance* (Bowling Green: Bowling Green University Popular Press, 1972), both by the author.

R. Serge Denisoff teaches at Bowling Green State University, Ohio, and is also the editor of *Popular Music and Society* and *Songs of Protest, War and Peace.*

church. One religious source which contributed to the "spontaneous songs" of social movements was the spiritual.

With the advent of the Civil War, spirituals were found with much more overt statements of protest than those which had gone before, stimulated by the conflict and the imminent prospect of freedom. Songs such as "Oh Freedom" and "No More Auction Block For Me" were sung by blacks who fought along with the Union Army. Then, shortly after the end of World War I, social movements began to take an interest in the spiritual. The use of religious music adds an appeal to tradition which social movements generally require. Movements, by their very nature of advocating social change, are generally not tied to tradition. Hymns, in part, appear to tie the movement to a national heritage, regardless of the programs they advocate. Finally, group singing encourages the individual to feel himself a part of the group or movement, and therefore important, allowing the participant to carry on.

Another important source of protest song was the labor college, organized to mobilize rural workers into the industrial union movement. Commonwealth Labor College in particular, which purchased a site in Mena, Arkansas in the late 1920s, made a contribution to the folk consciousness of the North. In the closing years of Commonwealth College, due to the influence of Claude Williams, a black preacher, the school began to borrow traditional folk songs, primarily spirituals, to communicate themes of social protest.

Williams had a great impact upon Lee Hays, who was later to perform in the Almanac Singers with Woody Guthrie and Pete Seeger. Hays transformed a number of hymns into secular messages of protest. After the closing of Commonwealth College in 1940, Lee Hays came north and injected many of the songs he learned at Commonwealth into the songbag of the Almanac Singers. An Almanac Singer credited a good portion of the group's approach to music to the pioneering efforts of Commonwealth College and particularly Claude Williams.

Another example of a labor school using native folk material for social and economic purposes is Highlander Folk School, which was a local enterprise created in 1932 in Monteagle, Tennessee. Mrs. Horton, the director of music in the school, collected and compiled 1,300 songs from unions, left-wing groups, and black and white southern tradition, and then disseminated these songs for organizational work. In all, the school published eleven songbooks, and their best-known song was "We Shall Overcome." This song

Songbook, *Negro Songs of Protest* by Lawrence Gellert, illustrated by Hugo Gellert, 1936, 7" × 10½" (Old Town School of Folk Music, Chicago)

was brought to Highlander by black Food and Tobacco Union workers, who had adapted it from the old church song "I'll Overcome Someday." Mrs. Horton introduced the song to gatherings throughout the south, and taught it to Pete Seeger in New York. Over the years other singers have added verses, and it continues to be a staple song of peace and freedom. The significance of the labor colleges is that they served as transfer points by which songs and personnel were directed from one movement to another.

The formation of the Almanac Singers marked the first organizational attempt to put folk consciousness into practice. The Almanacs both represented themselves as, and were lauded by their supporters as, the culmination of the so-called "folk tradition" or "folk memory" of the people. In December, 1940, a Harvard dropout named Pete Seeger joined with former Commonwealth College organizer Lee Hays for an appearance at the Jane Mountain Restaurant for the paltry sum of $2.50. From this inconspicuous beginning the group would expand in size and write approximately 200 songs on a plethora of subjects, most of which addressed the issues of trade unionism, political machinations in Europe, and the economy.

The Almanacs derived their name from the second most influential book in pre-industrial America, *The Farmer's Almanac*. The name was suggested by a phrase included in a letter written to Pete Seeger from Woody Guthrie. A fellow Almanac singer elaborated the purpose of the group: ". . . if you want to know what's good for the itch, or unemployment, or Fascism, you have to look in your Almanac. And that's what Almanac stands for" (Hays, Lee. "Almanacs: Part II." *People's Songs Bulletin* 3:9 (November 1948).

As the group increased in size, several teams of Almanacs began to appear simultaneously before different audiences. It is almost impossible to speak of one specific unit of Almanac Singers. Bob Claiborne in "Folk Music of the United States" described the group:

In 1940 all these influences were gathered together by the Almanac Singers. In and around this remarkable group were Lee Hays, once a Sharecropper's Union organizer; Woody Guthrie, folk poet of the "dustbowl" migrants; "Aunty Molly" Jackson, poetess laureate of the Kentucky miners; Elizabeth and Alan Lomax; . . . and more sophisticated musicians and writers like Pete Seeger, Millard Lampell and Earl Robinson. All had in common an active interest in folk music and its inherent democratic values.

On October 16, 1940, 16,500,000 men between the ages of twenty-one and thirty-five were registered according to the provisions of the Selective Service Training Act, the first peacetime military conscription in the nation's history. Congress passed this act in preparation for possible intervention abroad. One of the many songs which the Almanacs composed to protest this bill was "The Ballad of October 16th," set to the tune of "Jesse James":

Oh Franklin Roosevelt told the people how he felt,
We damned near believed what he said.
He said, "I hate war and so does Eleanor but
We won't be safe 'til everybody's dead."

When my poor mother died I was sitting by her side,
Promising to war I'd never go.
Now I'm wearing khaki jeans and eating army beans,
And told that J.P. Morgan loves me so.

Two years after the song's appearance the Almanacs were publicly sanctioned and discharged from the Office of War Information in part due to this song. In the anti-intervention campaign of 1939–40 the Almanacs recorded the album "Songs for John Doe," a three-record set, released in the spring of 1941, which is unfortunately no longer available. This set, which included "The Ballad of October 16th," contained six songs whose basic thesis was that the United States should remain neutral vis-à-vis the European conflict. This album contained numerous songs, such as "Plow Under," which appealed primarily to members of the American Peace Mobilization and other political organizations.

They said our system wouldn't work,
Until we killed the surplus off,
So now they look at us and say . . .

Plow the fourth one under, plow under,
Plow under, plow under
Plow under every fourth American boy.

Following the bombing of Pearl Harbor and the outbreak of World War II, however, the Almanacs' songs began to exhibit a militant patriotism previously absent from their work. In February of 1942 the Almanacs were attacked in the *New York Post* and in the *World Telegram*, which charged that the group, by compiling a songbook for the American Peace Mobilization and by performing antiwar songs at rallies, was disloyal and Moscow-oriented. These attacks in the New York papers were based on the group's par-

Album, 78 r.p.m., *Songs by Woody Guthrie*, Asch Records, 12″ × 10¼″ (Rick Steinberg)

90

ticipation in a "war morale" program. The accounts strongly objected to the appearance of the Almanacs on the same program with a message from President Roosevelt, in light of "The Ballad of October 16th." Any possibility of a recording contract was nullified by this newspaper report, and the group disbanded after the summer of 1942.

The contribution of the Almanac Singers to the recent folk music revival is not insignificant. The groups provided a form or structure for presenting folk music, i.e., trios, quartets, etc.

Portrait of Woody Guthrie, 24″ × 30″
(Folkways Records)

With the advent of the Cold War, a number of anti-war songs were written by People's Songs, Inc. and People's Artists, Inc. These two folksinging groups published magazines and songbooks which dealt with the topics of coexistence with the Soviet Union, nuclear war, and other issues. One of the better examples is Vern Partlow's "Talking Atomic Blues":

We hold this truth to be self-evident:
That all men may be cremated equal.

But the atom's international, in spite of hysteria,
Flourishes in Utah, also Siberia;
And whether you're white, black, red or brown,
The question is, when you boil it down:
To be or not to be . . . That is the question
Atoms to atoms and dust to dust . . .
If you listen to the money bags,
Somethin's bound to bust.

People's Songs Bulletin and *Sing Out!* are must periodicals for those interested in political peace songs. *Sing Out!* printed a vast number of anti-Korean policy songs during the time of the police action. One of the standard peace songs which emerged from this period was Ed McCurdy's "Strangest Dream." Part of the lyrics went as follows:

Last night I had the strangest dream,
I'd never dreamed before;
I dreamed the world had all agreed to put an end to war.

I dreamed I saw a mighty room,
The room was full of men,
And the paper they were signing
Said they'd never fight again.

A number of anti-war songs were popularized in the late 1950s and early 1960s with the coming of the folk music revival. Traditional pieces such as "Study War No More" were reintroduced, while newer songs of protest were composed. By then, folk music and protest music had their own recognized traditions and history. And although the issues and the songs change, the power of music to bring people together in the expression of their opinions has never been diminished.

Just a Song at Twilight:
Old Man Atom vs. the Cold War

VERN PARTLOW

A NOT SO FUNNY THING HAPPENED to me and my 1945 nuclear peace song, "Old Man Atom," on our way to the American public through the postwar twilight zone that had forever changed wars that could be "won" into wars that couldn't . . . .

The grimsy-whimsy "talking atomic blues" folksong with the prophetic Hirsoshima/Nagasaki wailing chorus, based on my interviews with nuclear scientists for the now defunct Los Angeles *Daily News* in the fall of 1945, made it to Tin Pan Alley with eight separate records high in the disc jockey charts in 1950.

Its commercial debut, thanks to Hollywood music publisher Irving Bibo, brought about rave trade magazine reviews, considerable media publicity, local and national radio and television interviews in whch I performed the song, and a reported "investigation" by military intelligence . . . .

At the peak of "Atom's" climb, when it was being played some forty times a day as a "request number" by New York radio jockeys, according to publisher Bibo, he was visited by a gent from the Pentagon.

Bibo phoned me to say that the man from military intelligence told him that "Atom" was very popular with American "police action" troops on armed services radio in Korea. The man, he said,

Perhaps peace had become offensive, but so was censorship.

Vern Partlow was a correspondent for the *Los Angeles Daily News* in the 1940s and '50s and is the composer of "Old Man Atom" or "The Talking Atomic Blues," one of the first popular anti-nuclear songs.

Vern Partlow. Photograph by
Eric Partlow.

wanted to interview me at the *Daily News*. I waited, but he never
came.

What did come, not much later, was an organized and virulent
attack on the song by hysterical Joe McCarthy types, who demanded of recording companies, music stores and radio stations
that "Atom" be "withdrawn" from circulation.

The targets of this unofficial censorship campaign chickened out
and obliged those who were charging that the song "echoed" the

94

then current Stockholm Peace Petition drive, which the attackers called "the Russian peace offensive." Perhaps those sneaky Swedes and Russians were "echoing" me and the atomic scientists who had actually inspired "Atom" five years earlier, a few months after the first manmade atomic fire exploded over two tragic noncombatant Japanese cities.

Perhaps peace had become offensive, but so was censorship . . . . Press reaction was instantaneous. Major editorials hit a wide variety of publications, chiding the music industry and airwaves for succumbing to threats and citing the First Amendment and reproducing key excerpts from the song:

"If Einstein's scared, I'm scared." "We hold this truth to be self-evident: all men may be *cremated* equal." "To be or not to be." "The atom's here to stay—but are we?" "The people of the world must choose between—the brotherhood of man, or smithereens." "Peace in the world, or the world in pieces."

BBC argued "Atom" could no longer be played on radio unless accompanied by a song expressing the opposition viewpoint. The jockeys couldn't fi one.

The Saturday Evening Post editorialized in 1950 that "Atom" was killed "apparently on the theory that people have become so hysterical that they are demanding a cheery attitude toward destruction." Yep—*some* people.

Life Magazine could find no "reason why any private group of censors should be allowed to keep the rest of the U.S. people from buying or refusing to buy a recording of Old Man Atom, if they choose." But the people weren't consulted . . . .

A *New York Times* editorial found the ban "a threat to freedom," "a new high in absurdity." It lashed out at the "sinister" and "alarming" willingness to "knuckle under to the slightest pressure" and the "cringing anxiety to avoid controversy, even though matters of principle are involved."

Deploring the successful censorial red-baiting of a peace song, the *Times* summed up succinctly: "If this sort of reasoning were followed to its logical conclusion, any book, play, song, speech or movie that opposed war, approved public housing, denounced Franco or praised caviar and borsch would be banned on suspicion of promoting Russian interests." But it wasn't a good year for logic.

As a lifelong newspaperman and hobbyist folksong singer and composer from Abe Lincoln country around Harris Station, Illinois (Pop. 31 on May 25, 1910, when I was born there), I knew that a

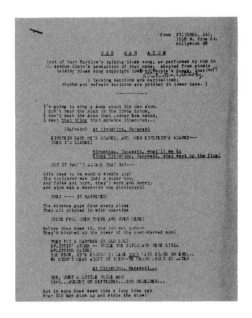

Manuscript, typed, "Old Man Atom," by Vern Partlow, 1945, 8½″ × 11″ (Vern Partlow)

good story or news event deserved a good song, up to and including the threat of a final-solution nuclear war.

What happened to "Atom" in that sad twilight period—the rhythmic plea for peace that Pete Seeger continues to call "the folksong of the atomic era"—was also happening to blacklist victims all over the country . . . .

Veritably, it seemed that thought control had not perished in that 1945 Berlin bunker but moved happily to the national capital of the "leader of the free world," where it was indeed alive and well, thanks to "loyalty oaths," the McCarthy brigades, etc. (Did Truman or anyone else really believe that a hardboiled Russian spy in the U.S. government or working in a "defense" plant would burst into tears and be forthwith defrocked in his trade because he could not "tell a lie"?). Well!

The rave reviews in *Billboard, Variety, Cash Box* and other music industry trade publications on the "Atom" recordings ceased. Decca Records' part-owner Bing Crosby stopped rehearsing his own surefire version; the Decca artists and repertoire man, who had auditioned me for an earthy follow-up album of OMA and other originals, titled "The Singing Newspaperman," told my publisher the attack on the song was crazy, but the company's stockholders, under the circumstances, could do without a "controversy." Moon and June still paid off and always would, it was decided.

Even so, "Old Man Atom" (sung, I seem to recall, with a full chorus and film clips of mushroom clouds, by Chicago's Win Stracke) was the featured finale at a pageant celebrating the city's centennial (I forget the date). The show included me and "Atom" because I am a native of Illinois, a former member of the Chicago United Press news bureau, and I guess somebody there identified with atomic survival.

I know I do. Any folk rock singers want to take another crack at it? Einstein, Oppenheimer, Szilard, Urey and I are still in our corner. I think the people of the world are increasingly in favor of "peace" over "pieces."

Joan Baez

Original Manuscript, typed and handwritten notes, Joan Baez' reaction to Kennedy assassination, November 22, 1963, 8½" × 11" (Joan Baez, Diamonds and Rust Productions)

Original Typed Carbon Copy, Joan Baez' letter to President Lyndon B. Johnson about Vietnam, February 14, 1965, 8½" × 11" (Joan Baez, Diamonds and Rust Productions)

Photograph, Joan Baez with Martin Luther King Jr., Grenada, Mississippi, 1966 (Joan Baez, Diamonds and Rust Productions)

Gold Record, presented to Joan Baez for album *Woodstock*, 1969, 12" × 12" (Joan Baez, Diamonds and Rust Productions)

Handbill, "Draft Age? Listen," anti-draft statement by Joan Baez on brown bonded paper, A.F.S.C., 8½" × 14" (Joan Baez, Diamonds and Rust Productions)

Original Manuscript, typed and handwritten notes for "Warriors of the Sun," 8½" × 11" (Joan Baez, Diamonds and Rust Productions)

Original Drawing, charcoal on newsprint illustration for song "All the Weary Mothers of the Earth," by Joan Baez, 1972, 19" × 24" (Joan Baez, Diamonds and Rust Productions)

Letter from Jimmy Carter, in admiration of Joan Baez' work, signed by Carter on White House stationary, "with love Jimmy," May 3, 1977, 6¾" × 9" (Joan Baez, Diamonds and Rust Productions)

Original Manuscript, handwritten on hotel room service card, lyrics for the song "Cambodia," 3½" × 5⅝" (Joan Baez, Diamonds and Rust Productions)

Letter and Certificate, from Theodore M. Hesburgh, National Cambodia Crisis Committee, presented to Joan Baez for her work on behalf of Cambodia, 8½" × 11" (Joan Baez, Diamonds and Rust Productions)

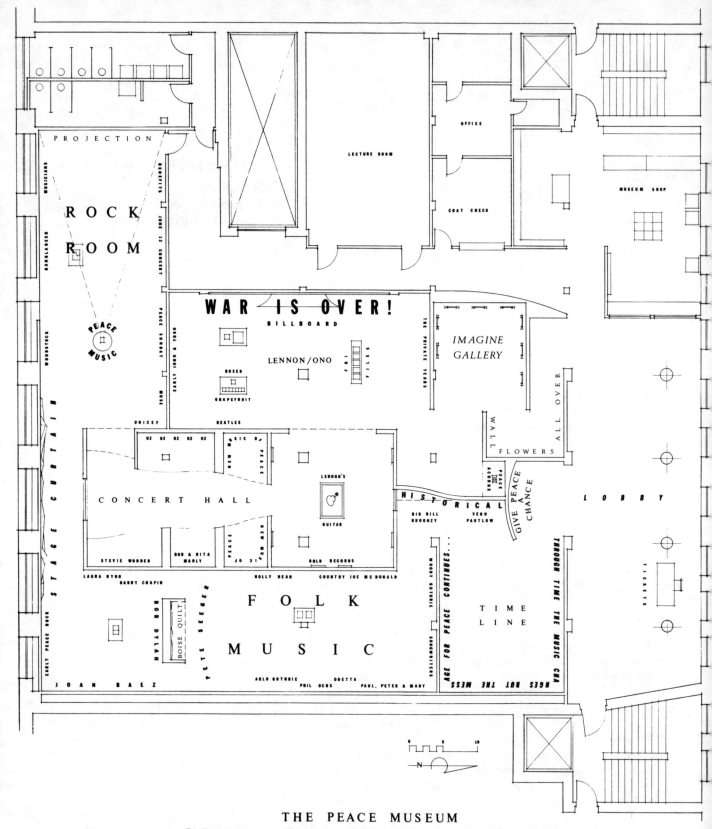

THE PEACE MUSEUM

GIVE PEACE A CHANCE

CHICAGO

MULLER & BROWN ARCHITECTS

CINCINNATI, OHIO

1983

The Beatles

Original manuscript, "The Word" by John Lennon and Paul McCartney, water color and ink on paper, 10" × 14", 1965 (Northwestern University Music Library)

Photograph, John Lennon by Richard Avedon, signed by photographer, 1968, 28" × 32" (Terri Hemmert)

Magazine, *The Beatles Are Here,* 1963, 8" × 11" (Jim McIntyre)

Harry Chapin

Award, Public Service Award/Rock Music Awards, to Harry Chapin for efforts on behalf of world hunger, 1976, 5⅜" × 11⅛" (Sandy Chapin)

Original manuscript, handwritten on notebook paper, "My Name is Jennifer," 1980, 8½" × 11" (Sandy Chapin)

Original manuscript, typed, "Remember When the Music", 1980, 8½" × 11" (Sandy Chapin)

Certificate, appointment to World Hunger Commission which Chapin lobbyed to establish, to Harry Chapin from Jimmy Carter, signed by Carter, September 12, 1978, 25" × 21" (Sandy Chapin)

Poster, Musical Tribute to Harry Chapin, with Steve Chapin, Tom Chapin, Pete Seeger, and others, various autographs, at Cornell University, February 5, 1982, 20" × 25½" (Sandy Chapin)

Bob Dylan

Photograph, Bob Dylan by Lisa Law, 1968 (Museum of Rock Art)

Photograph, Bob Dylan by Paul Natkin, 1982 (Photo Reserve)

Sing-Out Magazine, cover self-portrait by Bob Dylan, October–November 1968, 5½" × 8½" (Sing Out)

Sing-Out Magazine, cover photo of Bob Dylan, October–November 1962, 5½" × 8½" (Sing Out)

Handbill for series of six Dylan/Baez concerts scheduled for the fall of 1965, design by Eric von Schmidt, 5½" × 9½" (Manny Greenhill)

Early Historical Material

"A Mother's Plea for Peace: I Didn't Raise My Boy to Be A Soldier," (Brian/Piantadosi), 1915, 10½" × 13⅞" (Anonymous)

"After the War is Over, Will There Be Any 'Home Sweet Home'?" (Pourmon/Woodruff/Andrieu), 1917, 13¾" × 10½" (University of Illinois)

"Bring Back My Daddy to Me," (Tracey/Johnson/Meyer), 1917, 13¾" × 10½" (University of Illinois)

"Brother Bill Went to War While I Stayed at Home and Made Love to His Best Girl," (Branen/Lange), 1915, 13¾" × 10½" (University of Illinois)

"The Letter That Never Reached Home," (Leslie/Grossman/Gottler), 1917, 10¾" × 10½" (University of Illinois)

"When the Flag of Peace is Waving, I'll Return," (Meyer/Young), 1917, 13¾" × 10½" (University of Illinois)

Songbook, *Negro Songs of Protest* by Lawrence Gellert, illustrated by Hugo Gellert, 1936, 7" × 10½" (Old Town School of Folk Music, Chicago)

Songbook, *The People's Song Book*, Alan Lomax, 1948, 7" × 10½" (Old Town School of Folk Music, Chicago)

Newsletters, *People's Songs*, November 1947, May 1948, 8⅜" × 11" (Sing Out! Magazine)

Manuscript, typed, "Old Man Atom" by Vern Partlow, 1945, 8½" × 11" (Vern Partlow)

Arlo Guthrie

Book, *Alice's Restaurant*, soft cover, Grove Press, illustrated by Marvin Glass, 1966, 7" × 6¼" (Harold Leventhal)

Poster, one-sheet from movie *Alice's Restaurant*, 1969, 27" × 41"

Woody Guthrie

Album, 78rpm, *Songs by Woody Guthrie*, Asch Records, 12" × 10¼" (Rick Steinberg)

Photograph, portrait of Woody Guthrie, 24" × 30" (Folkways Records)

Sing Out!, Vol. 13 No. 1, "One Little Thing the Atom Can't Do," by Woody Guthrie, 5½" × 8½" (*Sing Out!*)

Songbook, *American Folksong: Woody Guthrie*, Oak Publications, 1961 (Old Town School of Folk Music, Chicago)

George Harrison/Bangladesh

Book, *I Me Mine*, George Harrison, 1979, 19½" × 10". Leather bound, special numbered edition, signed by George Harrison (Genesis Publications, England)

Program Booklet, The Concert for Bangladesh, 1972, 8" × 11" (Peter Hansen, U.S. Committee for UNICEF)

Poster, movie The Concert for Bangladesh featuring Eric Clapton, Bob Dylan, George Harrison, Ravi Shankar, Ringo Starr, 1972, 27" × 41" (National Screen Services)

Photograph, Bob Dylan and George Harrison, color, by Henry Diltz, 1972 (Museum of Rock Art)

June 12

Poster, "June 12 1982 March and Rally, Bread not Bombs" 18¾" × 25½" (Lee Nading)

Poster, "United Nations General Assembly Second Special Session on Disarmament" 1982, 25" × 19" (Lee Nading)

Poster, "March for Peace and Justice" June 12, 1982, 17" × 24" (Lee Nading)

Tom Lehrer

Original Manuscript, handwritten on staff paper, "Who's Next?" by Tom Lehrer, 1965, 8½" × 10¼" (Tom Lehrer)

Original Manuscript, handwritten on staff paper, "The Wild West Is Where I Want to Be" by Tom Lehrer, 1953, 9⅛" × 12¼" (Tom Lehrer)

Original Drawing, illustration by George Woodbridge for MAD Magazine spread on Tom Lehrer, 1957, 16⅝" × 9⅝" (Tom Lehrer)

"Tom Lehrer Sings About the Wild, Wild West," MAD Magazine, April 1957, 16" × 10¾" (Tom Lehrer)

Tom Lehrer Songbook, Crown Publishers, Inc., 1952, 7¼" × 10¼" (Old Town School of Folk Music, Chicago)

Lennon/Ono

Guitar, Gibson J 160 E, which John Lennon played while recording "Give Peace a Chance." Drawings and inscriptions by John Lennon 16" × 41¼" × 5" (Yoko Ono)

Single Record, "Give Peace a Chance/Remember Love," July 1969, 7" × 7¼" (J. V. McShirley)

Gold Record, "Live Peace in Toronto," December 1969, 21½" × 17" (Yoko Ono)

Peace Acorns, John Lennon and Yoko Ono sent a box of acorns and earth to major heads of state with a message asking that they plant them for peace, 1969, 5½" × 4" × 2" (Yoko Ono)

Gold Record, "Instant Karma," February 1970, 17½" × 13¼" (Yoko Ono)

Original Manuscript, handwritten and typed, John Lennon's letter to *Rolling Stone Magazine* about the Toronto Peace Festival, March 1970, 8½" × 11" (Jann Wenner)

Poster, "War is Over! If You Want It, Love and Peace from John & Yoko," 1971, 30½" × 20½" (Yoko Ono)

Poster, "John Sinclair Freedom Rally," featuring speakers Rennie Davis, Allen Ginsberg, Bobby Seale, Jerry Rubin, and others, and music by John Lennon, Yoko Ono, Archie Shepp, Roswell Rudd, Phil Ochs, Commander Cody, David Peel, and others, Ann Arbor, MI, 1971, 28" × 16" (Mike Rivers)

Grapefruit Box, conceptual art object by John Lennon and Yoko Ono, unfolds with objects inside, 1971, 6¼″ × 7¼″ × 6″ (Yoko Ono)

Gold Record, "Imagine," September 1971, 21½″ × 17″ (Yoko Ono)

Poster, "This is Not Here," signed by John Lennon and Yoko Ono, from exhibition at Everson Museum of Art, Syracuse, NY, October 1971, 18¼″ × 24¼″ (Yoko Ono)

Single Record, "Happy Xmas (War is Over)," first issue, written by John Lennon and Yoko Ono, December 1971, 7″ × 7¼″ (Yoko Ono)

F.B.I. Memos, photocopies, regarding John Lennon's immigration battle, 1972, 8½″ × 11″ (Jon Wiener)

Original Manuscript, John Lennon's thank-you note to *Rolling Stone Magazine* and readers after winning immigration battle, October 1975, 8½″ × 11″ (Jann Wenner)

Poster, "Double Fantasy," 1980, 48″ × 50″ (Yoko Ono)

Cartoon, original art by Doug Marlette, "Pick the Public Figure the F.B.I. Did Not Spy on for Illegal Activities . . .," 1983, 23″ × 14¼″ (Doug Marlette, *Charlotte Observer*)

Cartoon, original art by Doug Marlette, "Wanted by the F.B.I.," 1983, 14½″ × 23″ (Doug Marlette, *Charlotte Observer*)

Bob Marley

Photograph, Bob Marley by Bob Gruen, 1982 (Bob Gruen, Radius Graphics)

Photograph, "One Love" peace concert poster, photo by Peter Simon, 1978 (Timothy White)

Photograph, Bob Marley at "One Love" peace concert bringing together Jamaican Prime Minister Michael Manley and leader of the opposing Jamaican Labour Party Edward Seaga to shake hands in a public expression of unity, photo by Kate Simon, April 22, 1978 (Timothy White)

Stamps, issued in Jamaica commemorating Bob Marley, photographs on stamps by Rita Marley, issued 1981, 1″ × 1½″ each (Doug Schimmel)

Country Joe McDonald

Photograph, Country Joe at the Moscone Vietnam Veterans Benefit, San Francisco, by Jackie Frapp, 1982 (Country Joe McDonald)

Newspaper article, "Country Joe Takes a Wife," describes Country Joe's wedding, San Francisco Express Times, April 4, 1968, 16″ × 22½″ (Florence McDonald)

Poster, Moscone Benefit for Vietnam Veterans (Country Joe McDonald, Jefferson Starship, Grateful Dead, Boz Scaggs), May 28, 1982, 14¼″ × 22¼″ (Vietnam Veterans Project)

Record, "Resist," Side 1, "Kiss My Ass," "Tricky Dicky"; Side 2, "Free Somebody" released by Entertainment Industry for Peace and Justice, cover design by Jane Fonda, Recorded in the San Francisco Bay Area July 1971, 7½" × 10⅜" (Country Joe McDonald)

Holly Near

Mailgram, from Tom Hayden about Holly Near's participation in the Indochina Peace Campaign, December 4, 1974, 8½" × 11" (Holly Near and Redwood Records)

Pamphlet, "The Indochina Peace Campaign: A Working Paper by Tom Hayden," March 1973, 7" × 10¾" (Holly Near and Redwood Records)

Original Manuscript, typed and handwritten, "No More Genocide," words and music by Holly Near, 1982, 8½" × 11" (Holly Near and Redwood Records)

Paper Necklace, of origami peace cranes, presented to Holly Near at anti-nuclear demonstration, 11" long (Holly Near and Redwood Records)

Poster, The Indochina Peace Campaign presents Jane Fonda, Tom Hayden, Holly Near, 16" × 9¾" (Holly Near and Redwood Records)

Poster, Unite Our Struggles—Chile and the U.S. with Holly Near and Alive, music in solidarity with the women of Chile, February 4, 1978, 17" × 24¾" (Holly Near and Redwood Records)

Poster, Holly Near: Songs of Victory & Struggle, benefit concert for Chile and Vietnam, by Women's Coalition for Chile, February 24, 1978, 12" × 16" (Holly Near and Redwood Records)

Poster, No More Genocide In My Name, in opposition to nuclear weapons, November 15, 1978, 17½" × 30" (Holly Near and Redwood Records)

Poster, The FTA Show, (Free The Army) with Jane Fonda, Donald Sutherland, Holly Near and others, 1971, 23" × 35" (Holly Near and Redwood Records)

Laura Nyro

Original Manuscript, handwritten song lyrics, ink on construction paper, "Child of the Universe", 1978, 12" × 16½" (Laura Nyro)

Original Manuscript, handwritten song lyrics, ink on construction paper, "Mother's Spiritual", 1983, 12" × 17½" (Laura Nyro)

Original Manuscript, handwritten song lyrics, ink on construction paper, "The Right to Vote", 1983, 12" × 17½" (Laura Nyro)

Phil Ochs

Original Manuscript, typed and handwritten, "Chaplain of War," words and music by Phil Ochs, 1966, 19⅛" × 12" (Mike Ochs)

Original Manuscript, handwritten on TWA flight stationary, "Death of the American," 7¼" × 9" (Mike Ochs)

Poster, Friends of Chile Presents An Evening With Salvador Allende, with Phil Ochs, Arlo Guthrie, Pete Seeger, and others, Madison Square Garden, May 9, 1974, 11" × 17" (Mike Ochs)

Letter, from Representative Phillip Burton to Phil Ochs regarding his participation in Broadway for Peace, February 1, 1968, 7" × 8⅞" (Mike Ochs)

News Release, regarding the first "War is Over" celebration organized by Phil Ochs, November 16, 1967, 8½" × 11" (Mike Ochs)

Poster, "The War Is Over!," Central Park, May 11, 1975, 23" × 29" (Don Luce)

Odetta

Photograph, Odetta at Seva Foundation benefit, 1982, by Lisa Law, (Museum of Rock Art)

Poster, Summer Soltice [sic] Celebration, benefit for American Indian Movement, Syracuse, NY, June 22, 1983, 17" × 33" (Holly Near and Redwood Records)

Tom Paxton

Original Manuscript, handwritten in spiral notebook, "Born on the Fourth of July," words and music by Tom Paxton, May 1976, 16" × 10" (Tom Paxton)

Poster, Glastonbury CND Festival featuring Tom Paxton, Curtis Mayfield, The Chieftans and others, June 17th, 18th, 19th, 1983, 25" × 17½" (Campaign for Nuclear Disarmament, England)

Peace Sunday

Program Booklet, Peace Sunday "We Have A Dream", June 6, 1982, 10¾" × 8¼" (Lisa Law)

Schedule of Peace Sunday acts, handwritten, 4' × 5', 1982 (Mac Holbert)

Backstage passes to Peace Sunday, June 6, 1982, 12⅛" × 16⅛" (Mac Holbert)

Award, "1st Annual Woody Guthrie Humanitarian Award to Graham Nash for your Outstanding Contribution Toward Peace and a Nuclear Free Future, presented by Southern California Alliance for Survival," November 18, 1982, 10" × 14" Graham Nash)

Original Manuscript, Graham Nash's early notes on Peace Sunday, pencil and ink on notebook paper, January 19, 1982, 8" × 11" (Graham Nash)

Peter, Paul and Mary

Photograph, portrait by Lisa Law, 1963 (Museum of Rock Art)

Photograph, portrait by Paul Natkin, 1982 (Photo Reserve)

Poster, *Reunion* album, 1978, 23½″ × 35″ (Warner Brothers)

Songbook, *The Best of Peter, Paul and Mary, Ten Years Together,* Pepamar Music Corp.,1970, 9″ × 12″ (Carl Fischer Music, Chicago)

Songbook, *Recorded Hits of Peter, Paul and Mary,* Pepamar Music Corp., 1962, 9″× 12″ (Carl Fischer Music)

Malvina Reynolds

Original Manuscript, handwritten on staff paper, "From Way Up Here," words by Malvina Reynolds, music by Pete Seeger, 1962, 8½″ × 9⅜″ (Schroder Music)

Original Manuscript, handwritten on staff paper, "The Plutonium Song," words and music by Malvina Reynolds, 1975, 14″ × 9½″ (Schroder Music)

Handbill, Benefit Concert for People Against Nuclear Power featuring Malvina Reynolds, 1977, 8½″ × 11″ (Schroder Music)

Poster, Musical Celebration with Friends of Malvina Reynolds, tribute to Malvina Reynolds, (Pete Seeger, Country Joe McDonald, Steve Goodman, and others), May 18, 1978, 19″ × 24″ (Schroder Music)

Paul Robeson

Photograph, Robeson at Paris "Peace" Parley with W.E.B. DuBois and James Crowthe, by Rene Henry, AP Photo, April 22, 1949

Album Cover, "Robeson Sings," 33⅓ rpm, includes spirituals, Hassidic chant, Russian folk song, no date, 10¼″ × 10¼″ (Rich Steinberg)

Album Cover, "Songs of Free Men," 78rpm, includes from Russia, Spain, Germany, no date, 12″ × 10³⁄₁₀″ (Rick Steinberg)

Album Cover, "Ballad for Americans," 78rpm, music by Earl Robeson, lyrics by John Latouche, no date, 12″ × 10½″ (Rick Steinberg)

Pete Seeger

Original Manuscript, typed with handwritten notations, "A True Story: How 'Waist Deep in the Big Muddy Finally Got on Network Television in 1968," by Pete Seeger, 1983, written for The Peace Museum (Pete Seeger)

Pete Seeger Peace Quilt, 9′ ×9′, 1983 (Boise Peace Quilt Project)

Original Manuscript, with note to manager Harold Leventhal, "One Man's Hands," words by Dr. Alex Comfort, music by Pete Seeger, 1962 (Harold Leventhal)

105

Photo reproductions of original handwritten manuscripts for "If I Had a Hammer" 1950, "We Shall Overcome" 1960, "One Man's Hands" 1962, "Waist Deep in the Big Muddy" 1966 (Harold Leventhal)

Photograph, by Dave Gahr of Pete Seeger at Newport Folk Festival, with Joan Baez, Bob Dylan, Peter, Paul and Mary, New Freedom Singers, 1963 (Dave Gahr)

U2

Picture disc, *War*, 1983, 12″ × 12″ (Island Records)

Flag, U2 War, 1983, 11″ × 17½″ (Terri Hemmert)

Stage backdrop from 1983 U.S. tour (Ellen Darst)

Stevie Wonder

House Resolution 800, legislation seeking Martin Luther King's birthday as national holiday, January 1983, 7½″ × 11″ (Rep. John Conyers)

Poster, Join Stevie Wonder, January 15, 1982, MLK National Holiday March, Washington D.C., 16⅞″ × 22″ (Black Bull Music)

Photomural, Stevie Wonder at piano, photo by Lisa Law, 1982 11′ × 7′ reproduction (Lisa Law)

Woodstock

Japanese "Woodstock" tickets, for Japanese version of Woodstock concert which never happened, 1969, 2½″ × 7″ each (Museum of Rock Art)

Poster, Woodstock Music and Art Fair Presets an Aquarian Exposition, Three Days of Music and Peace, White Lake, N.Y., 1969, designed by Arnold Skolnick (Arnold Skolnick)

A Brief Guide
to Music for Peace:
A Bibliography/Discography

CLINTON F. FINK

Music expressing opposition to war and a desire for peaceful human relations comes in many forms. Song is the most common, and one may find peace themes in all kinds of songs—hymns, folk, popular, blues, gospel, rock, reggae, or art songs. Larger vocal works are also represented—choral works, cantatas, oratorios, operas, operettas, and musical comedies. Even instrumental works, in classical, popular, and jazz idioms, have been intended by their composers to express sentiments for peace.

Some of these works, and the musicians and writers responsible for them, are listed below under three main headings—songs, larger vocal works, and instrumental works. The lists are based on a search in many different sources. They cover mainly, but not exclusively, 20th century American music. This guide is selective, and thus incomplete. It is intended to provide an introduction, and perhaps stimulate further exploration of the fascinating variety of ways in which musicians have contributed to the quest for peace.

SONGS. The songs are listed here by author or occasionally by a performing group. Dates indicate when the song was written or first published. If the song listed is known to have been written earlier than the publication in which it was found, the date is preceded by the symbol "<". Other symbols and abbreviations which follow some song titles indicate that the writer is responsible only for the words (w), the music (m), an adaptation (adapt), a translation (w-Engl), an arrangement (arr), or for collecting a folk song (coll).

Some of the songs have new words written to an older tune that was not necessarily a peace song until the new words were written. In such cases, the name of the original tune or its composer is given after the new song title, but the composer is not listed separately. In the reverse case, where an older poem or text has been set to music, the name of the poet or the text is given after the song title, and is not listed separately.

Abraham Lincoln Brigade. Peat bog soldiers (1934)

Accad, Evelyne. Dans la Plaine, elles avancent/On the plain, they advance (1975); Il n'y a plus de soleil/There is no more sunshine (1975); Je veux vivre/I want to live (1976); Je t'aime et des hommes meurent/I love you and men are dying (1977); Quand elle est venue/When she came (1977); Il suffrait d'un mot peut-être/Perhaps it would be enough (1978); Leila, une jeune femme revolutionnaire/ Leila, a young revolutionary woman (1978); Nous allons la reconstruire/We will rebuild it (1978); Une ville qui meurt dechirée/A city that dies torn apart (1979); La ville est en flammes/The city is in flames (1980); Nous avons une ville à rappiécer/We have a city to patch up (1981).

Adams, Derroll. Portland town (1957)

Allan, Lewis. I saw a man (w, 1919?)

Almanac Singers. Strange death of John Doe (w, 1940s; m = "Young man wouldn't hoe corn")

Altman, Shalom. Vine and fig tree (w-adapt, < 1966; m = traditional)

Anderson, Donnie. Peace (1975)

Anderson, Laurie. O Superman

Anderson, Robert. Peace (1975)

Andrisse, Jim. Beautiful planet (1982); Just a blue-green ball (1982).

Andrieu, Harry. After the war is over (m, 1917)

Angulo, Hector. Guantanamera (m-adapt, 1963; m, Jose Marti)

Arkin, David. The dove (w, 1962)

Armitage, Marie Teresa. Psalm of peace (w, 1916; m, Beethoven); Blessed are the peacemakers (m, 1916; w, The Beatitudes).

Arnold, Linda. Mothers for disarmament (1980s); No place to hide (1980s); Power to heal (1980's); Sweet mother earth (1980s); Won't this be a fine place (1980s).

Atinsky, Jerry. Peace march song (1962)

Axton, Hoyt. Joy to the world (1970)

Baah, A. K. Stand up and fight back (1978)

Bacharach, Burt. What the world needs now is love (m, 1965)

Backer, B. I'd like to teach the world to sing (1971)

Bacon, Michael. The ballad of William Penn (1975)

Bacon, Josephine Daskam. Hymn for the nations (w, 1934; m = Beethoven, "Ode to Joy")

Baez, Joan C. Saigon bride (m, 1967); Here's to you (w, 1971); All the weary mothers of the earth (1972); Song of Bangladesh (1972); Where are you now, my son? (1973); Where's my apple pie? (1974); For Sasha (1979); Cambodia (1980); Warriors of the Sun.

Baker, Henry. O God of love (w, 1861; m, 1866)

Balderson, Steve. A miracle and a mountain (1982)

Batchellor, Daniel. The dawn of peace (m, 1909); The banner of peace (m, 1910).

Baum, M. Louise. Peace (w, 1927; m, Beethoven)

Bax, Clifford. Turn back, o man (w, 1919; m, L. Bourgeois, 1551)

Beckett, Larry. No man can find the war (1967)

Benet, W. C. A hymn of peace (w, 1914; m = "Hursley")

Bentley, Eric. Peace song/ Friedenslied (w-Engl, 1964; m, H. Eisler); Ballad of the soldier/Ballade vom soldaten (w-Engl, 1955; m, H. Eisler).

Berns, Ruth. La guerre est finie/ The war is over (< 1967)

Binkerd, Gordon. Peace
(m, 1968)

Blane, Ralph. Pass that peace pipe
(1943)

Blakeslee, Dick. Passing through
(1953)

Bode, A. Keep us, o Lord
(w, 1916; m, Beethoven)

Bogle, Eric. The band played
Waltzing Matilda (1977); The
green fields of France.

Bowie, David. Fantastic Voyage
(1979), It's No Game, He-
roes, Beauty and the Beast

Brecht, Bertolt. Ballade vom sol-
daten/Ballad of the soldier
(w, 1930s); Friedenslied/Peace
song (w,1930s).

Brel, Jacques. Les flamandes/Mar-
athon (1959); La colombe/The
dove (1960); Bruxelles/
Brussels (1962); Au suivant/
Next (1968); Quand on n'a
que l'amour (1968); Les toros/
The bulls (1968).

Brigham, Robert. Song of union
(w, 1925; m, Beethoven)

Brooker, Gary. Conquistador
(m, 1967); Fires which burnt
brightly (m, 1973).

Brooks, Mary. The Jack Ash Society (w, 1961)

Brown, Francine. The deserter/Le
deserteur (w-Engl, 1950s)

Browne, Jackson. Before the
Deluge

Brunner, John. The H-bomb's
thunder (w, 1958;
m = "Miner's lifeguard")

Bryan, Alfred. I didn't raise my
boy to be a soldier (w, 1915)

Buckley, Tim. No man can find
the war (1967)

Burke, Jos. A. The hero of the
European war (1916)

Burdon, Eric. Sky Pilot (1968,
The Animals)

Burnaby, Davy. The conscientious objector's lament
(ca. 1915)

Bush, Belle. The banner of peace
(w, 1910)

Caesar, Irving. Child of all nations (1946); Fifty friendly
nations (1946); Hallelujah!
bless the peace (1946); How
to spell friendship (1946);
Let's make the world of tomorrow today (1946); Song
of the good neighbor (1946);
This is our last chance for
peace (1946); United Nations
(1946); We'll soon be one
world (1946).

Campbell, Paul (i.e., The
Weavers). Glad tidings
(w, 1951; m = "Shalom
chaverim")

Carman, Bliss. Lincoln's land
(w, 1925?)

Carmichael, Hoagy. Inbrothered
(m, 1947?; w, Edwin Mark-
ham)

Carmines, Al. Peace anthem
(1969)

Carter, Sidney. Crow on the cradle (1962)

Chapin, Harry. Circle; Cat's in
the Cradle

Chaplin, Ralph. Commonwealth
of toil (w, 1918; m = "Darling Nelly Gray")

Chicago Freedom Movement.
Never too much love (1963)

Church, Mabelle Carolyn. My
big little soldier boy
(m, 1915)

Claiborne, Bob and Adrienne.
Listen Mr. Bilbo (w, 1946;
m = traditional)

Clash, The (Joe Strummer, Mick
Jones, Paul Simonon).
Straight to Hell; Washington
Bullets; The Call-Up; Charlie
Don't Surf; Rebel Waltz; Hate
and War (1977); London Call-
ing (1979); Spanish Bombs;
The Guns of Brixton; English
Civil War (1978); Ivan Meets
G.I. Joe

Cleary, Ann and Marti. Stron-
tium 90 (1959)

Cliff, Jimmy. Sufferin' in the land
(1969); Vietnam (1969); Won-
derful world, beautiful people
(1969); Stand up and fight
back (1978); Universal love
(beyond the boundaries)
(1978).

The Colonel. Too Many Cooks
in the Kitchen

Comfort, Alex. There's rain in
the forest (w, 1960s;
m = "The cruel wars");
Go limp (w, 1962; m =
"Sweet Betsy from Pike");
One man's hands (w, 1962);
Ban, ban, ban the bloody
H-bomb (w, < 1966; m
= "John Brown's body");
I'm not going to be the
unknown soldier (<
1966).

Converse, Frederick Shepherd.
Farewell, old year
(m, < 1915)

Conway, Bob. Another side of
engineering (w, 1977;
m = Peggy Seeger, "I'm
gonna be an engineer")

Cook, R. I'd like to teach the
world to sing (1971)

Cooper, Charles E. I wish the
war was over (m, 1902)

Corti, Jean. Les toros/The bulls
(m, 1968)

Costello, Elvis. Goon squad (1978); Oliver's army (1978); Senior service (1978).

Cousins, D. Martin Luther King's dream (1978)

Crabtree, Peter. It ain't really true (w, 1963; m = "My darling Nelly Gray")

Crawford, Bob. When there's peace on earth again (1917)

Crews, William D. Adieu to militarism (1917)

Crosby, Stills, Nash & Young. Woodstock; For What It's Worth; Teach Your Children

Cui, Cesar. War (m, 1917)

Cunningham, (Agnes) Sis. An anthem for the space age (1962); Do Russian people stand for war (w-Engl, < 1969)

The Cure. Boy's Don't Cry

Dallas, Fred. The family of man (< 1964)

Dallas, Karl. Doomsday (w, < 1966; m = "St. James infirmary blues"); The family of man.

Dane, Barbara. It isn't nice (m, 1964)

Darnell, Shelby. Gee, mom, I want to go home (1950)

David, Hal. What the world needs now is love (w, 1965)

Davies, Ray. Yes sir No sir (1969); Uncle Son (1971); 20th Century Man (1971)

Davis, B. I'd like to teach the world to sing (1971)

Davis, Lionel B. If we die (m, 1978; w, Ethel Rosenberg)

Day, George Henry. Not alone for mighty empire (m, 1942; w, W. P. Merrill, 1909)

The Dead Kennedys. Holiday in Cambodia; Police Truck; Bleed For Me

DeFrange, Tim. For them to keep (1982); God save us from ourselves (1982); Leave my DNA alone (1982).

DeFrange, Tom. Alice's song (1982); Garden to grow (1982); The last protest song (1982); The prime minister's oratory (1982).

DeKoven, Reginald. Recessional (m, < 1913; w, Rudyard Kipling)

DeLange, Eddie. Peace, brother (w, 1939)

Ditchik, Ralph. Song for peace (m, < 1961)

Dodge, Corinne B. Peace (w, 1915)

Dolmatovsky, E. Song for peace (w, < 1953)

Dubin, Alfred. The hero of the European war (w, 1916); The dream of a soldier boy (w, 1917).

Dusheck, Nina. Saigon bride (w, 1967)

Dyer-Bennet, Richard. Passive resistance (1945)

Dykes, John B. O brother man, fold to thy heart (m, 1875; w, John G. Whittier, 1848)

Dylan, Bob. Blowin' in the wind (1962); Masters of war (1963); Train a-travelin' (1963); With God on your side (1963); Gates of Eden; A hard rain's a-gonna fall; It's alright ma, I'm only bleeding; Talking World War III blues; The times they are a-changin'.

Dykema, Peter W. The olive tree (m-arr, 1947?; Greek folk tune)

Eastwood, Clint. Can't take another world war (1981)

Eisler, Hanns. Ballade vom soldaten/Ballad of the soldier (m, 1930s); Friedenslied/Peace song (m, 1930s).

Elbert, Charles. We'll build a little home in the U.S.A. (m, 1915)

Enola Gay. Orchestral Manoeuvers in the Dark

Farrell, Russ. Then we'll have peace (< 1966)

Fay, Stephen. Peace be with all (w, 1926?; m = traditional Lithuanian)

Fiske, Stephen Longfellow. An actual survivor (1982); Bridges of love (1982); The choice (1982); Peacemakers (1982); Radiation (1982); Stop the insanity! (1982).

Flanders, Michael. Twenty tons of TNT (1967); The reluctant cannibal (< 1977); Song of patriotic prejudice (< 1977); The ostrich (< 1977).

Fox, C. Milligan. Mistress Magrath (m-coll + arr, 1915; traditional Irish tune)

Frederick, Bill. Talking peace (1963); Way of the dinosaur (1964); And freedom too (1965); Cold War calypso (1965).

Friedman, Jim. In the hills of Shiloh (m, 1963)

Friesen, Agnes. The shelter diggers (w, 1962; m, W. Guthrie, "Buffalo skinners"); Will you work for peace or wait for war? (1962).

Gaines, Samuel Richard. Brotherhood (1926?)

Gang of Four. I Love a Man in a Uniform; He'd Send in the Army

Garrett, Lee. Peace (there must be peace) (w, 1975)

Geddes, Shareen. Ageless winds of time (1982); Hiroshima (1982)

Geldof, B. (I never loved) Eva Braun (1979?)

The Generals. The Damned

Gibson, Kate. Time will bring peace and you, dear (w, 1918)

Gilmore, Patrick. When Johnny comes marching home (w, 1860s; m = traditional Irish)

Glazer, Tom. United Nations make a chain (Hold on) (w, 1946; m = "Mary had a golden chain"); The whole wide world around (because all men are brothers) (w,1947; m, H. Hessler/J. S. Bach); CARE (Official song of CARE, Inc.) (1949); Black man fights wid de shovel (coll + arr, 1967; Afro-American folk song from World War I); I don't want to be a soldier (coll + arr, 1967).

Glover, Henry. Red's dream (1962)

Goldberg, Sam. Michael (1949; w, R. Service, 1921)

Gordon, Irving. Two brothers (1951)

Gorney, Jay. The four rivers (m, < 1969)

Gorton, Ruthie. Oh my beautiful friends (1973)

Gottler, Archie. The letter that never reached home (m, 1916)

Grant, Annie McVicar. The blue bells of Scotland (w, 1927?)

Graves, Alfred P. Mistress Magrath (w-revised, 1915; m = traditional Irish)

Greenleaf, Phillis. Alive, alive, oh (w, 1982?; m = "Cockles and Mussels"); Take me out of this war game (w, 1982?; m = "Take me out to the ball game").

Grice, Roy. Then we'll have peace (< 1966)

Grinnell, O. S. We are all Americans (1914); The blue and the gray (< 1914).

Grossman, Bernie. The letter that never reached home (w, 1916)

Guthrie, Arlo. Alice's Restaurant massacree (1967?); Neutron bomb song.

Guthrie, (Woodrow Wilson) Woody. I've got to know (w, 1950; m = "Farther along"); Put my name down (m, 1950); This land is your land (1956); Better world a-coming (1963); Peace call (1963); One little thing the atom can't do (1963).

Hadley, Henry. America (m, 1915?)

Hall, John and Johanna. Children's cry (1982)

Hall, John P. Don't forget that he's your president (1916)

Haney, Lynn Mary. Peace sign (1975)

Harburg, E. Y. The same boat, brother (w, 1945?)

Harmon, Frank. Peace (1975)

Harley, Steve. White, White Dove (1976) G. I. Valentine (1976)

Harrison, George. Bangla Desh (1971); Give me love (give me peace on earth) (1973).

Hays, Lee. Hammer song (w, 1950); Tomorrow is a high-way (w, 1950); Wasn't that a time (1957); The war is over/ La guerre est finie (w-Engl, 1967).

Hellerman, Fred. Come away Melinda (m, 1963)

Heaven 17. (We Don't Need This) Fascist Groove Thang

Hidaka, Tadashi. In that cursed morning of Hiroshima (1966)

Hill, Joe (Joseph Hill-ström). Don't take my papa away from me (1915); Stung right (1915?).

Hille, Waldemar. The dove (m, 1962)

Holler, Dick. Abraham, Martin, and John (1968)

Holmes, John Haynes. God of the nations, near and far (w, 1911; m, J. Walch, 1860)

Holmes, Oliver Wendell. God bless our fatherland (w, < 1913; m = "America")

Hoppin, Stuart Bliss. Massasoit (m, 1947?)

Horton, Zilphia. We shall over-come (coll, 1936; m = Afro-American hymn)

Hosmer, Frederic Lucien. Hear, o ye nations (w, 1909; m, F. J. Haydn)

Hughes, Billy. Atomic sermon (ca. 1953)

Ince, Thomas H. Peace song (w, 1916)

Ingram, Luther. Respect yourself (1971)

Jackson, Jill. Let there be peace on earth (1955)

Jackson, Joe. Battle Ground (1980)

Jaffe, Judah A. War (w, 1917)

Jam, The. "A"-Bomb in Wardour Street; The Eton Rifles; Little Boy Soldiers; Funeral Pyre

Jefferson, Blind Lemon. Wartime blues (1917)

Jethro Tull. War Child

John, Elton. The Border Song (1969) Talking Old Soldiers (1970)

Johnson, Bill. Atom and evil (1946)

Johnson, Howard. Bring back my daddy to me (w, 1917)

Johnson, J. Rosamund. Lift every voice and sing (m, 1900)

Johnson, James Weldon. Lift every voice and sing (w, 1900)

Jones, Matthew. Hell, no! I ain't gonna go (1968)

Jones, Mick. English civil war (1978?); Guns on the roof (1978?); Tommy gun (1978?); London calling (1979?); Spanish bombs (1979?).

Jouannest, Gerard. Bruxelles/Brussels (m, 1962; see J. Brel)

Kadish, Gene. The submarine called Thresher (1963)

Keller, Matthias. Angel of peace (m, 1915?; w, O. W. Holmes)

Kendrick, John F. Christians at war (w, < 1916; m = "Onward Christian soldiers")

Kent, Enoch. Man with the knob (w, 1962; m = "The man that waters the workers' beer"); The pigeon (w, < 1966; m = "The sour milk cairt").

Kerr, Harry D. I'm an American—that's all (w, 1915)

Kevess, Arthur. Thoughts are free/Die gedanken sind frei (w-Engl, 1950; m = traditional German); Ariran (w, 1950; m = traditional Korean).

King, Frankie ("Pee Wee"). (I'm praying for the day that) Peace will come (1944)

King Krimson. 21st Century Schizoid Man; Peace—A Beginning; Peace—An End

The Kinks. Uncle Son (1971) Yes Sir, No Sir (1969)

Kirby, Fred. Atomic power (1945)

Kittredge, Walter. Tenting tonight (on the old campground) (1860s)

Klickman, F. Henri. Uncle Sam won't go to war (1914)

Kolmanovsky, E. Do Russian people stand for war? (m, < 1969)

Koschat, Thomas. Peace (m, 1925?; w, from the Bible)

Kramer, Aaron. Song for peace (w, 1961?)

Kretzer, Leo. Spirit sun (1974); Power game (1975).

Kulisiewicz, Alexander. Die lebenden steine/The living stones (m, 1943)

LaFarge, Peter. Take back your atom bomb (< 1969)

Langley, Jeff. Broken promises (m, 1975)

Lanier, Sidney. America (w, 1915?)

Laron, Elaine. Hell no! I ain't gonna go (1968)

Lehrer, Tom. The wild west is where I want to be (1953); It makes a fellow proud to be a soldier (1958?); We will all go together when we go (1958); MLF lullaby (1964); National brotherhood week (1964); The folk song army (1965); Send the marines (1965); So long, mom (1965); Wernher von Braun (1965); Who's next? (1965).

Lems, Kristin. Don't tread on me (1976); Such a world (1976); The 50s sound (1978); Too cheap to meter (1979); Circles of sunlight (1983); Where do the animals go? (1983).

Lennon, John. Revolution (1968); Give peace a chance (1969); Imagine (1971); Happy Christmas (War is over); Hard times are over; I don't want to be a soldier; Mind Games; Sunday, Bloody Sunday; Gimmie some truth.

Leslie, Edgar. The letter that never reached home (w, 1916)

Levy, Mark. Save the black hills; Talkin' raw deal; Who builds the H-bomb? (1980)

Lewis, Roger. When there's peace on earth again (1917)

Lingard, William Horace. Captain Jinks (w, 1860s)

Lowe, Nick. What's so funny 'bout peace, love, and understanding (1978) American Squirm

Lowenfels, Walter. Wasn't that a time (1957)

M. Official Secrets; Your Country Needs You

MacColl, Ewan. Brother, won't you join in the line (w, 1960; m = traditional American); The dove (w, 1962; m = traditional); Five fingers (w, 1962; m = traditional Scots); That bomb has got to go (w, 1963; m = traditional sea chantey); Furusato (w-English verse, < 1966; m, I. Astu, 1940s)

Mackagan, T. Captain Jinks (m, 1860s)

Maitland, Don. The golden rule (w, 1925?)

Manley, Frederic. Farewell, old year (w, < 1915)

Marley, Bob & Rita. Exodus; Judge Not; Children of the Ghetto

Martens, Frederick Herman. The brotherhood of man (w, 1915?; m, D. F. E. Auber); Let dread war cease (w, 1915?; m, G. F. Händel).

Martin, Hugh. Pass that peace pipe (1943)

McCartney, Paul. Give Ireland Back to the Irish

McConnell, George B. The hero of the European war (1916)

McCurdy, Ed. (Last night I had the) Strangest dream (1950)

McDade, Carolyn. Singin' praises (1975); America (1979); I am enraged (1979); With whom do you stand? (1979); Coming home (1980); Peace at last (1980); Ballad of the rivers (1981); I hear some voices calling (1981); Song of hands (1981)

McDonald, Country Joe. I-feel-like-I'm-fixin'-to-die rag (1968); An untitled protest (1968); The call (m, 1971; w, R. W. Service, ca. 1920); Forward; Jean Desprez; The man from Aphabaska; The march of the dead; The munition maker; The twins; War

widow; Young fellow my lad (all songs 1971, musical settings of poems by Robert W. Service); The Agent Orange Song; A Vietnam Veteran Still Alive

McLean, Will. Freedom train (1963)

Mendelssohn, Felix. How lovely are the messengers (1836, from the oratorio, "Saint Paul").

Merrill, Blanche. We take our hats off to you, Mr. Wilson (1914)

Meyer, George W. Bring back my daddy to me (m, 1917)

Meyer, Mary Ruth. When the flag of peace is waving I'll return (w, 1917)

Miller, Sy. Let there be peace on earth (1955)

Minkoff, Fran. Come away Melinda (w, 1963)

Mitchell, Chuck. The peaceful sound (1982?)

Monaco, James V. The dream of a soldier boy (m, 1917)

Moody Blues. Lost in a Lost World

Moore, Jessie Eleanor. Round the world (Abendruh) (w, < 1955)

Morricone, Ennio. Here's to you (m, 1971)

Morrison, Ellen. In thy peace (1975); Surely he taught us (1976).

Morrison, Jim. The peace frog (1970); The Unknown Soldier (1968)

Motors. Nightmare Zero

Mouloudji. Le deserteur (1950s)

Myers, Henry. The four rivers (w, < 1969)

Nash, Graham. Military Madness

Nathan, Casper. Uncle Sam won't go to war (1914)

Near, Holly. Better days (1972); Birthday children (1972); G. I. Movement (1972); No more genocide (1972); Hang in there (1973); Oh America (1973); Wedding song (1973); It could have been me (1974); Broken promises (1975); Ain't nowhere you can run; Foolish notion; Hay una mujer desaparecida (1978?); Take it with you wherever you go; Wrap the sun around you; Family promise

Nelson, Bill. Panic in the World (1977, Be Bop Deluxe)

Nesbit, Wilbur D. My big little soldier boy (w, 1915)

Newman, Randy. Political Science

Nile, Willie. Now that the war is over (1975)

Nilsson, Harry. Ambush; Old Forgotten Soldier

999. Soldier

Nyro, Laura. Save the country (1968); Brown earth (1971); Christmas in my soul (1971); Mothers Spiritual (1983).

Ochs, Phil. Celia (1963); How Long? (1963); Lou Marsh (1963); Talking Cuban crisis (1963); Talking Vietnam (1963); There but for fortune (1963); The Thresher (1963); Draft dodger rag (1964); I ain't marchin' anymore (1964); One more parade (1964); This old world is changing hands (1964); Cannons of Christianity (1965); Santo Domingo (1965); Cops of the world (1966); Is there anybody here? (1966); White boots marchin' in a yellow land (1966); (I declare) The war is over (1968); When in Rome (1968); I kill, therefore I am (1971).

Ogden, Althea A. A song of peace (1909, written for the Second National Peace Congress, Chicago, May 1, 1909)

Ono, Yoko. John, John, Let's Hope For Peace; Remember Love; We're All Water; I See Rainbows (1982)

Osby, Rev. Woke up this morning with my mind set on freedom (w, 1960s; m = traditional).

Oxenham, John. In Christ there is no East or West (w, 1908; m, A. R. Reinagle, 1836); Peace in our time, o Lord (w, < 1941; m, G. J. Elvey, 1868).

Page, Jim. Hiroshima Nagasaki Russian Roulette (1976)

Paley, Claudia. Lament of the soldier's wife (w, < 1966; m = traditional)

Paperte, Frances. Universal prayer for peace (1959)

Partlow, Vern. Talking atom(ic blues) (1947)

Paxton, Tom. Six men riding (1962); Strange rain (1962); There was a time (1962); What did you learn in school today? (1962); When morning breaks (1962); A rumbling in the land (1963); The thresher disaster (1963); Train for Auschwitz (1963); The willing conscript (1963); I read it in "The Daily News" (1964); Lyndon Johnson told the nation (1965); Peace will come

(1972); Talking Vietnam potluck blues; Born on the Fourth of July (1977); Mister Blue/White bones of Allende (1977).

People's Songs. United Nations make a chain (w, 1946; m = "Mary had a golden chain")

Piantadosi, Al. I didn't raise my boy to be a soldier (m, 1915)

Pierpont, Victor. The golden rule (m, 1925?)

Pinard, Sir Lancelot. Walk in peace (1946)

Pink Floyd. The Post-War Dream; Us and Them; The Gunner's Dream; Two Suns in the Sunset

The Pop Group. A Will . . .

Pourmon, E. J. After the war is over (w, 1917)

Powers, Chet. Get together (C'mon people now smile on your brother) (1963)

The Professionals. Join the Professionals

Puebla, Carlos. Guajira por Lolita Lebrón (1975)

Random Hold. The March

Reed, Daniel. Windham (m, 1700s)

Refior, Everett. One world (w, 1970s?; m = "This land is your land")

Reid, Keith. Conquistador (w, 1967); Fires which burnt brightly (w, 1973).

Reis, Pat. One world soon (1979)

Reig, Teddy. Red's dream (1962)

Repaid, Billy. Once more he is our president (1916)

Reynolds, Malvina. We hate to see them go (1959); From way up here (w, 1962); I

want to go to Andorra (1962); What have they done to the rain? (1962); The wise men (1962); The boy salutes (1963); It isn't nice (1964); Playing war (1964); Singin' Jesus (1964); Bitter rain (1965); The bloody neat (1965); I believe (1965); The man says jump (1965); Peace isn't treason (1965); Ring like a bell (w, 1966); The Saigon children (1966); A short history of warfare (1966); The albatross (1968); World in their pocket (1975).

Reynolds, Tim. Peace anthem (w, 1967/69)

Rice, Gitz. The conscientious objector's lament (ca. 1916); I want to go home (1917).

Rice, Les. (I can see) A new day (1962)

Rice, Mack. Respect yourself (1971)

Rich, Charlie. Peace on you (1974?)

Ritchie, Jean. None but one (1972)

Roberts, Ellwood. The dawn of peace (w, 1909)

Robinson, Earl. The same boat, brother (m, 1945?); Spring song (m, 1930s)

Rodney, Winston (Burning Spear). Throw down your arms (1970s)

Rogers, James H. Great peace have they which love thy law (m, 1908; w, Psalms).

Rolfsen, Nordahl. O God of hosts (w, 1915?; m, E. Grieg)

Ross, Gertrude. Peace (m, 1915)

Rothery, W. G. The bells of Aberdovey (w, 1926?; m = traditional Welsh)

Russell, Bob. He ain't heavy—he's my brother (1969)

Russotto, Leo. m-arr for songs by Irving Caesar

Sadot, Joseph M. Prisoners of war (1973)

Saint, General. Can't take another world war (1981)

Sainte-Marie, Buffy. The universal soldier (1963); Now that the buffalo's gone (1964); My country 'tis of thy people you're dying (1966); The seeds of brotherhood (1967); Soldier blue (1970).

Sanders, Betty. Song for peace (w-Engl, < 1953)

Sands, T. All the little children (1970s?)

Santly, Joseph. When there's peace on earth again (1917)

Sawyer, Charles C. When this cruel war is over (w, 1860s)

Schacter, Harry. Spring song (w, 1930s/1953)

Schermerhorn, M. K. Song of peace (Forward all ye faithful) (w, 1890s; m = A. Sullivan, "Onward Christian soldiers")

Schertzinger, Victor L. Peace song (m, 1916)

Schimmel, Nancy. Mack the bomb (w, < 1966; m = K. Weill, "Mack the knife")

Schultz, Ferdinand. Round the world (m, < 1955)

Sciver, Esther Van. Gee, mom, I want to go home (1950)

Scott, Bobby. He ain't heavy— he's my brother (1969)

Scott-Heron, Gil. Save the children; We almost lost Detroit; The Revolution Will Not Be Televised

Seeger, Peggy. The crooked cross (1960); There's better things

to do (w, 1960; m = traditional American); That bomb has got to go (w, 1963; m = traditional sea chantey); Please Mr. Reagan (1982?).

Seeger, Pete. Hammer song (If I had a hammer) (m, 1950); Tomorrow is a highway (m, 1950); Oh had I a golden thread (1959); Where have all the flowers gone (1961); Flowers of peace (w, 1962; m = "Will ye go, lassie, go?"); From way up here (m, 1962); I want to go to Andorra (m, 1962); One man's hands (m, 1962); Turn! turn! turn! (m-adapt, 1962; w = Ecclesiastes 3:1-8); All mixed up (1965); Don't you weep after me (w, < 1966; w + m, traditional); Ring like a bell (m, 1966); Waist deep in the big muddy (1966); If you love your Uncle Sam, bring them home (1968); We Shall Overcome (arr).

Shaw, Vincent. Time will bring peace and you, dear (m, 1918)

Sherman, Richard M. and Robert B. It's a small world (1963)

Shostakovitch, Dmitri. Song for peace (m, < 1953)

Silber, Irwin. Put my name down (w, 1950); Song for peace (w-Engl, < 1953).

Silverman, Jerry. Candy (m-arr, 1952); Passing through (m-arr, 1953).

Silverstein, Shel. In the hills of Shiloh (w, 1963)

Simmonds, James. The Ulster soldier boy (< 1966)

Simon, Paul. 7 o'clock news/silent night (1966); Peace like a river (1971); Armistice day (1972).

Simonon, Paul. The guns of Brixton (1979?); Guns on the roof (1979?).

Singer, Lou. I want to live in a friendly world (m, 1949); 'Round the world polka (m, 1949); U.N. alphabet song (m, 1949); U.N. Charter song (m, 1949); We're building a happier world (m, 1949).

Sloan, P. F. Eve of destruction (1965)

Small, Fred. No more Vietnams (1981)

Smith, David Stanley. Centennial hymn (m, 1876?; w, J. G. Whittier)

Smith, I. T. America's prayer for peace (w, 1940; m = "America")

Smith, Marion. Massasoit (w, 1947?)

Smith, Marvin. Peace (There must be peace) (1975)

Snow, Henry. Ode to joy (w-Engl, from Schiller, < 1916; m, Beethoven)

Sourire, Soeur, O. P. Dominique (1962)

Sparks, Randy. Dominique (w-Engl, 1962)

Spaulding, Hector. Lincoln's land (m, 1925?)

Speaks, Oley. Thou wilt keep him in perfect peace (m, 1913; text from Isaiah, Psalms)

Special AKA. War Crimes

The Spizzles. Risk

Spoelstra, Mark. The times I've had (1962); We've got to find another way (1962); Civil defense sign (1963).

Star Jets. War Stories

Stevens, Cat. Peace train (1971)

Stevens, David. Politeness (m, 1915?); The olive tree (w, < 1947; m = traditional Greek).

Stevens, Ray. Everything is beautiful (1970)

Stielstra, Jay. Leave the bottle on the table, waiter, I ain't finished yet (1974); American son (1982); Jimmy's war (1982).

Stone, Lloyd. A song of peace (w, 1934; m, J. Sibelius, from "Finlandia", 1865)

Stotts, Stuart. The man in the hood (for the work of Amnesty International (1982); Nuke free zone (1982); 3½ tons of T.N.T. (1982); Viet vet (1982); Vote for the freeze (1982); World citizen (1983).

Strange, (Poor Boy) Michael. The ballad of Martin Luther King (1968)

Strummer, Joe. English civil war (1978?); Guns on the roof (1978?); Tommy gun (1978?); London calling (1979?); Spanish bombs (1979?).

Student Nonviolent Coordinating Committee (SNCC). We're gonna move (1965); We shall not be moved (w-adapt, 1960s; music = traditional Afro-American); Woke up this morning with my mind set on freedom (w, 1960s; m = traditional).

Swann, Donald. Pilgrim's plea for peace, truth, and unity (1968)

Swift, L. E. There are three brothers (< 1948)

Symonds, John Addington. These things shall be—a loftier race (w, 1880; m = "Duke Street")

Taylor, James. Children's cry (1982)

Temple, Sebastian. Prayer of Saint Francis (1967)

Thomas, Edith Lovell. The world one neighborhood (m-arr, 1935; from Praetorius, 1610)

Tracey, William. Bring back my daddy to me (w, 1917)

Travaline, Dominick. Let the red, white and blue alone (1914)

Tucker, Harry. When this cruel war is over (m, 1860s)

U2 (Bono Vox, The Edge, Adam Clayton, Larry Mullen). Sunday, Bloody Sunday; New Years Day

Van Heusen, Jimmy. Peace, brother (m, 1939)

Vaughan, Henry. Peace (w, 1968)

Virginia Journal of Education. The coming day of peace (w, < 1913; m = "Battle hymn of the republic")

Vories, William Merrill. Let there be light (w, 1908; m, W. Boyd, 1868)

Watts, Isaac. Windham (w, 1700s)

Wells, Jenny. I saw a man (m, 1919?)

Wesley, Howard. We'll build a little home in the U.S.A. (w, 1915)

West, Don. Hymn for the nations (w-new verse, 1966; original w, J. D. Bacon)

Whitmore, Katherine. Let peace endure (w, 1926?)

Wickes, Ed. M. I wish the war was over (w, 1902)

Wilkie, Colin. The victors; Where were you in the war? (< 1982).

Williams, David. Nuclear power blues (1970s)

Williams, Hank (Sr.). (I'm praying for the day that) Peace will come (1944)

Williams, Theodore C. When thy heart, with joy o'erflowing (w, 1891; m, E. W. Bullinger, 1874)

Williams, Tom. Do Russian people stand for war? (w-Engl, < 1969)

Williams, W. R. We stand for peace while others war (1914)

Wolfe, Paul. Talking Christmas (1963)

Wolff, Bill. What a grand and glorious feeling (w, < 1966; m = "Oh how lovely is the evening")

Wonder, Stevie. Happy Birthday; Front Line

Wood, Albert. Candy (1952)

Woodruff, Jos. After the war is over (w, 1917)

Woods, Nick. Peace of mind (1967)

XTC. Generals and Majors; Sgt. Rock

Yarrow, Peter. The cruel war is raging (1961)

Yevtushenko, Y. Do Russian people stand for war? (w, < 1969)

Young, Barney G. When the flag of peace is waving I'll return (m, 1917)

Young, Neil. Ohio

Zaret, Hy. I want to live in a friendly world (w, 1949); 'Round the world polka (w, 1949); U.N. Alphabet song (w, 1949); U.N. Charter song (w, 1949); We're building a happier world (w, 1949).

Songbooks on Peace

Many peace songs can be found in anthologies of peace songs or in books or anthologies with special sections of peace songs. These are listed below.

A Hymnal for Friends (Philadelphia: Friends General Conference, 1955).

Anderson, Maragarite. *Beautiful bugles of peace* (Washington, D.C.: H. Kirkus Dugdale, 1912).

Andrews, Fannie Fern (comp.). "Selections for Peace Day", in *The Promotion of Peace* (Washington, D.C.: United States Bureau of Education, *Bulletin*, 1913, No. 12, pp. 48–57).

Bausch, Michael; Duck, Ruth. *Everflowing Streams* (NY: Pilgrim, 1981).

Boeckel, Florence Brewer (comp.). "Songs", in her *Across Borderlines* (Washington, D.C.: National Council for Prevention of War, 1926. pp. 141–5).

—————. "Songs to sing", in her *Through the Gateway* (Washington, D.C.: National Council for Prevention of War, 1926. pp. 101–103).

Glazer, Tom (comp. and ed.). *Songs of Peace, Freedom, and Protest* (NY: David McKay, 1970).

Hille, Waldemar, *et al* (eds.). *The People's Song Book* (NY: Boni and Gaer, 1948).

"Hymns for Peace Meetings" (Boston: American Peace Society, 1906).

Kettel, A. (comp.). *Wir wollen Frieden für alle Zeiten: Neue and alte Friedenslieder/We Want Peace for All Time: New and old peace songs* (Dortmund: Pläne, 1982).

Sheldon, John (ed.). *The Quaker Song Book* (London: Stainer & Bell for the Quaker Fellowship of the Arts, 1981).

Silber, Irwin (ed.). *Lift Every Voice: The Second People's Song Book* (NY: People's Artists, 1953).

Silva, Katherine E. *Peace Collection* (Silva, 1975).

Student Peace Union (comp. and ed.). *Songs for Peace* (NY: Oak, 1966).

Songs of the Spirit (Philadelphia: Friends General Conference, Religious Education Committee, 1978).

Whitman, Wanda Willson (ed.). *Songs That Changed the World* (NY: Crown, 1969).

Other Songbooks

Other songbooks include peace songs, even though there is no special section devoted to peace. Most of the collections listed below have been consulted in compiling this guide.

Armitage, Marie Teresa (ed). *Junior Laurel Songs*, Teacher's Ed. (Boston: C. C. Birchard, 1916).

—————. *Folk Songs and Art Songs* (Boston: C. C. Birchard, 1925).

—————. *Senior Laurel Songs*, Teacher's Ed. (Boston: C. C. Birchard, 1926).

Baez, Joan. *The Joan Baez Songbook* (NY: Ryerson, 1964).

Carawan, Guy and Candie. *Freedom is a Constant Struggle* (NY: Oak, 1963).

Collins, Judy. *The Judy Collins Songbook* (NY: Grosset & Dunlap, 1969).

Cunningham, (Agnes) Sis (comp. and ed.). *Broadside: Songs of our times from the pages of Broadside Magazine*, Vol. 1 (NY: Oak, 1964).

Dyer-Bennet, Richard. *Richard Dyer-Bennet: The 20th century minstrel* (NY: Leeds, 1946).

Dykema, Peter W., *et al* (eds.). *Sing Out! A singing school* (Boston: C. C. Birchard, 1947).

Giddings, Thaddeus P., *et al* (eds.). *Three-Part Music* (Boston: Ginn, 1925).
——————. *Two-Part Music* (Boston: Ginn, 1927).
Gospel Rock (Miami: Screen Gems/Columbia, 1974).

Happening Hits (Westbury, NY: Cimino, 1970s).

I.W.W. Songs: To fan the flames of discontent (Cleveland: I.W.W. Publishing, 1916).

Landeck, Beatrice (comp. & ed.). *"Git on Board": Collection of folk songs arranged for mixed chorus and solo voice* (NY: Edward B. Marks, 1950).
Lomax, Alan; Guthrie, Woody; Seeger, Pete. *Hard Hitting Songs for Hard Hit People* (NY: Oak, 1947).
Love—For Everyone (Miami: Screen Gems/Columbia, 1972).

1001 Jumbo Song Book (NY: Charles Hansen, 1970s).

Peter, Paul, and Mary: A collection (NY: Pepamar, 1968?).

Silber, Irwin (comp. and ed.). *American Hootenanny, Books 1 and 2* (NY: Consolidated, 1964).

Silber, Irwin, *et al* (eds.). *Reprints from Sing Out! The Folk Song Magazine, Vols. 1–9.* (NY: Oak, 1960–1966).
Silverman, Jerry. *Folk Song Encyclopedia,* 2 Vols. (NY: Chappell, 1975).

200 Superstar Song Hits (Hollywood, CA: Almo, 1978).

Van Ronk, Dave; Ellington, Richard (eds.). *The Bosses' Songbook: To stifle the flames of discontent* (Cooper Station, NY: Richard Ellington, 1959).

The Weavers (Ronnie Gilbert *et al*). *The Weavers Song Book* (NY: Harper & Row, 1960).

Larger vocal works

Peace themes also occur in vocal works other than songs. The following list presents a sample of choral works, cantatas, oratorios, operas, operettas, and musical plays. The works are listed alphabetically by composer. Other information given includes the lyricist or librettist (if other than the composer) or the texts used in the piece, the date of composition or publication of the work, recordings, and indications of the type of work and its content.

Alter, Martha *Peace* (Chorus for women's voices; text from Bacchylides; 1940)
Arne, Thomas *Hush to Peace* (A cappella chorus; NY: Lawson-Gould/G. Schirmer, 1958)
Arnell, Richard *The War God* (Cantata; text by Stephen Spender; 1944)

Bach, Johann S. *Peace Be Unto Israel* (Chorus, edited by Walter E. Buszin; Concordia Publishing House)

Bergel, Peter *Dr. Atomic's World-Famous Medicine Show* (Musical comedy; traveling show, c/o Peter Bergel, CALS, P.O. Box 12763, Salem, OR, 97309)
Binder, Abraham Wolfe *The Road To Peace* (Operetta for children, 1936)
Britten, Benjamin *War Requiem, op. 66* (Oratorio; text from the Missa pro Defunctis and the poems of Wilfred Owen; vocal score by Imogen Holst; commissioned for the festival

to celebrate the consecration of St. Michael's Cathedral, Coventry, May 1962; piano-vocal score published in London by Boosey & Hawkes, 1962; recorded on Klavier KS544, 1975)
Brunswick, Mark *Lysistrata* (Ballet suite for orchestra, chorus of women's voices, and mezzo-soprano solo; text from Aristophanes; 1936)
Bryan, Charles Faulkner *King of Peace* (Cantata, 1941)

Carmines, Al *Peace* (Musical based on Aristophanes' "Peace"; book and lyrics by Al Carmines and Tim Reynolds; New York: Caaz Music/Chappell, 1969)

Casals, Pablo *Hymn to the United Nations* (Chorus; text by W. H. Auden; NY: Alexander Broude)

Caron, Allan *A Prayer for Peace/ Priere pour la paix* (Anthem for mixed voices; French text by Paul Rovert; Winnipeg: Mello-Music, 1950)

Converse, Frederick S. *The Peace Pipe* (Cantata for mixed voices, with baritone solo and orchestra; text from Longfellow's "Hiawatha"; Boston, C. C. Birchard, 1915)

Damrosch, Walter *The Dove of Peace: Comic opera in three acts* (Vocal score arranged by A. W. Lilienthal; NY: G. Schirmer, 1912)

DeFrange, Tim: DeFrange, Tom *Alice in Blunderland: Reflections of a nuclear age* (A contemporary musical allegory; Cuyahoga Falls, OH: Legacy, Inc., 1982)

Etler, Alvin *Peace Be Unto You* (Anthem for Easter or general use, for four-part mixed chorus a cappella; text from St. Augustine's Prayer Book and Matthew 28: 1–10; NY: Associated Music, 1959)

Frangkiser, Carl *A Prayer for Peace* (Chorus for mixed voices, from "Dedication"; NY: Belwin, 1941)

Glass, Philip *Satyagraha* (Opera concerning the life of Gandhi and the development of his philosophy of nonviolence; 1980)

Gordon, David *The Peace Child* (musical) 1982

Hoffman, Lilburne *A Prayer for Peace* (Choral arrangement of music by Cesar Franck; text by Donald R. Frederick; to the memory of Raymond A. Hoffman; Wichita, Kansas: Raymond A. Hoffman Co., 1951)

Huss, Henry Holden *Winged Messengers of Peace* (Chorus; NY: G. Schirmer, 1937)

Joubert, John *Pro Pace Motets* (For a cappella chorus; recorded Borough Green, Sevenoaks, Kent: Novello, 1970s)

Lehrer, Tom *Tomfoolery* (Musical revue of his songs, including several anti-war songs; first performed in London, 1980; original cast album appeared in London, MMT LP001, 1980)

Lems, Kristin *Catch it on the Run* (Musical revue of her songs, including several peace and antiwar songs; first performed in Urbana, IL, June 1983)

Leonard, Clair *Prayer for Peace/ Priere Pour La Paix* (For mixed chorus with organ or piano accompaniment; text from the Episcopal Prayer Book; Boston: Boston Music, 1940/1944)

Livezey, Jan *Bang* (Musical about the dangers of nuclear war; Washington, D.C.: Washington Peace Center, 1982)

McLin, Lena Johnson *The Torch Has Been Passed* (A cappella chorus; based on a text by John F. Kennedy concerning the achievement of world peace; 1960s)

O'Hara, Geoffrey *One World* (Choral arrangement by Harry R. Wilson; text by John W. Bratton; NY: Bourne, 1945)

———— *Prayer for Peace* (Choral arrangement by Marcel G. Frank; text by Richard Wolfe; NY: Murbo/Bourne, 1965)

Pimsleur, Solomon *Fight Against War and Fascism, Op. 37* (Cantata for mixed chorus and piano; 1936)

———— *Anthem for Doomed Youth, Op. 38, No. 2* (Chorus for men's voices and harmonium; 1937)

———— *Pageant of War Sonnets, Op. 51* (Oratorio; 1943–45)

Powell, John *Soldier, Soldier— Folk Song* (A cappella chorus with soprano and baritone solos; NY: J. Fischer and Brothers, 1936)

Powell, Laurance *A Song of Peace* (chorus; 1943)

Prokofiev, Sergei *War and Peace, Op. 91* (Opera in 13 scenes after the novel by Leo Tolstoy; Libretto by Sergei Prokofiev and Mira Mendelson-Prokofieva, 1941; piano-vocal score by L. T. Atovmyan, Moscow 1973; recording, Columbia/Melodiya M4 33111, 1974)

———— *On Guard for Peace, Op. 124* (Oratorio, 1950; text by Samuil Yakovlevich Marshak; recorded by Melodiya/ Seraphim S-60067, 1960s; in this oratorio Prokofiev endeavored to express his feelings on war and peace, and his firm belief that there will be no more wars—that all nations of the world will safeguard peace and save civilization, our children, our future)

Road Less Travelled (Doug Krehbiel, Jude Krehbiel, Emory Wedel) *Please Freeze* (Musical variety show about the nuclear arms race and efforts to stop it; traveling show, c/o Mennonite Voluntary Service, Box 347, Newton, KS 67114)

Rogers, Bernard *The Warrior* (Opera, 1946)

Rorem, Ned *War Scenes* (Suite for solo voice and piano; text drawn from Walt Whitman's diary of the Civil War, *Specimen Days,* 1882; dedicated "to those who died in Vietnam, both sides, during the composition; 20–30 June, 1969"; first performed by Gerard Souzay with pianist Dalton Baldwin, in Constitution Hall, Washington, D.C., October 19, 1969)

Schafer, Raymond Murray *Threnody: For youth choir, youth orchestra, five narrators, and electronic music* (Cantata; text from accounts of the atomic bombing of Nagasaki; Scarborough, Ontario: Berandol Music, 1970)

Schönberg, Arnold *Friede auf Erden/Peace on Earth Op. 13* (For mixed chorus, a cappella or with small orchestra; text by Conrad Ferdinand Meyer; English translation by Arthur Fagge; composed 1907; published by Tischer and Jagenberg, 1912; new revised edition, London: Schott and Co., 1955; recorded on *The Choral Music of Schönberg,* Everest SDBR 3182, 1968)

Smith, Gregg *Beware of the Soldier* (Choral work; text from various sources, including St. Francis, Mark Twain, Leo Tolstoy, Thomas Hardy; recorded on Composers Recordings CRI SD341, 1975)

Strafford Open Forum *Button, Button, Who's Got the Button? . . . A Dream of Nuclear War* (Large scale community play/pageant with music; South Strafford, VT: Strafford Open Forum, 1982?)

Talma, Louise Juliette *Voices of Peace* (For mixed chorus and strings; text from The Missal, The Bible, St. Francis of Assisi, Gerard Manley Hopkins; 1973)

Thompson, Randall *The Peaceable Kingdom* (A sequence of sacred choruses for unaccompanied mixed voices; text from the prophecy of Isaiah; commissioned by the League of Composers for the Harvard Glee Club and the Radcliffe Choral Society, G. Wallace Woodworth, Director; Boston: E. C. Schirmer, 1936)

Ward, William R. *A Prayer for Christian Unity* (For mixed choir; text by Molly Anderson Haley; NY: Edward B. Marks, 1957)

Warner, Richard *Prayer for the Family of Nations* (Chorus; text from the *Book of Common Prayer;* dedicated to Merle Andregg, Director, and First Methodist Choir, Kent, Ohio; Boston: C. C. Birchard, 1956)

Williams, Ralph E. *Era of Peace* (Anthem for chorus; NY: Bourne, <1965)

Instrumental works

Although it is more difficult to express pro-peace or anti-war sentiments through strictly instrumental music, it is not impossible. Many composers have done so through the titles, dedications, or program notes for particular works. A brief sample of such works follows. The list is divided into three sections: piano or organ solos, orchestral or ensemble works, and jazz pieces. The listing is by composer, with other information (dates, publications, recordings) provided when it is available.

Piano or Organ Solos

Alford, Harry L. *The Peacemaker: Two Step* (March dedicated to Theodore Roosevelt for calling the peace conference that ended the Russo-Japanese War; Chicago: Will Rossiter, 1905)

Blon, Franz Von *Sounds of Peace: March, Op. 34* (London/NY: Hawkes and Son/Joseph W. Stern, 1902)

Born, Karl *Die Waffen Nieder: Welt-Friedens-Marsch/Lay Down Your Arms: World Peace March, Op. 120* (Bremen: W. Peterin, 1890s)

Dellafield, Henry *Dawn of Peace* (March dedicated to Andrew Carnegie for his philanthropic efforts on behalf of the peace movement; 1913)

Engelmann, H. *Message of Peace: Reverie* (Philadelphia: Jos. Morris, 1905)

Farwell, Arthur *Song of Peace* (From "Impressions of the Wa-Wan Ceremony"), *Op. 21, No. 7* (Newton Center, MA: Wa-Wan Press, 1906; reprinted in John Gillespie, *Nineteenth-Century American Piano Music,* NY: Dover, 1978)

Gould, Morton *Prologue—1945* (Dedicated to the San Francisco Conference of the United Nations; NY: Mills Music, 1945)

Graham, Irene *Peace Waltz/Centennial Peace Waltz* (1975)

Hamilton, Iain *Threnos: In Time of War* (Organ solo; I-Dawn, II-Holocuast, III-Elevation, IV-Purgatory and Requiem; commissioned by Marilyn Mason for her recital in Westminster Abbey as part of the 900th anniversary celebrations; Bryn Mawr: Theodore Presser, 1970)

Harthan, Hans *Peaceful River Waltzes* (Philadelphia: Joseph Morris, 1908)

LaCalle, Jos. *Peace Forever: March and Two Step* (Union Mutual Music, 1899)

Rucks, Robert Jerome *Peace and Harmony* (1975)

Scott, James *Peace and Plenty Rag* (St. Louis: Stark Music, 1919; reprinted in Rudi Blesh, *Classic Piano Rags,* NY: Dover, 1973)

Slaughter, Donald *The Peace Suite* (1975)

Vandersloot, C. M. *Peace Conference March* (Dedicated to Theodore Roosevelt for calling the peace conference which ended the Russo-Japanese War; Williamsport, PA: Vandersloot Music, 1905)

————— *Palace of Peace: March Two Step* (In honor of the opening of the Peace Palace at the Hague; Williamsport, PA: Vandersloot Music, 1914)

Williamson, Malcolm *Peace Pieces: Books I and II* (Organ solo; I-Peace in Childhood, II-Peace in Youth, III-Peace in Soli-

tude, IV-Peace in America, V-Wise Men Visit the Prince of Peace, VI-The Peace of God That Passeth All Understanding; London: Josef Weinberger, 1972)

Orchestral, Band, or Ensemble Works

Alexander, Joseph *Peace Overture* (Orchestral score, 1960s)

Fiorillo, Dante *One World* (Incidental stage music, 1945)

Forsberg, Charles William *Discantus Pacem* (Original composition for Ph.D., University of Minnesota, 1973)

Iannaccone, Anthony *The Prince of Peace* (Original composition for Ph.D., University of Rochester, 1973)

Jackson, Bruce Rogers *Quartet, in Memoriam for the Dead and Dying of Vietnam* (1978)

Kepner, Fred *Forward for Peace* (March written for the second inauguration of President Dwight D. Eisenhower, and premiered in the 1957 inaugural parade by Col. George S. Howard and the U.S. Air Force Band; Summy Publishing, 1957)

Klohr, John N. *R. H. Peace and Progress* (March written before 1956; recorded by the U.S. Navy Band on the album "Heritage of the March" a salute to America's Bicentennial, 1976)

Maganini, Quinto *Peaceful Land* (Orchestral score, 1945)

Orland, Henry *Peace* (NY: 1971)

phony Orchestra on Philips PH S2-901, 1956)

Strube, Gustav *Peace Overture* (Orchestral score, 1945)

Teixeira, Tony *A Peace Piece* (Boston: Berklee Stage Band Series, 1973)

Penderecki, Krzysztof *To the Victims of Hiroshima: Threnody for 32 String Instruments* (Recorded by the Warsaw National Philharmonic Sym-

Still, William Grant *The Peaceful Land* (1950s; this composition won a first prize from the National Federation of Music Clubs)

Wood, Morgan *Dona Eis Requiem (For the Victims of My Lai)* (1970s)

Jazz

Most of the following works appear only on recordings. They are listed according to the artists who recorded them, with the name of the piece given first, then the name of the composer in parentheses, then information about record albums.

Ayler, Don "Peace" on *In Florence 1981* (Frame Records, RF-2001/2/3, 1982)

Baker, Chet "Peace" (H. Silver) on *Peace* (Munich: Enja Records 4016, 1982)

Beirach, Richard See D. Liebman

Coltrane, John "Peace on Earth" (J. Coltrane, 1966) on: *Infinity* (Impulse 9225); *Concert in Japan* (Impulse 9246-2); *Mastery of John Coltrane, Vol. 3* (Universal City, CA: MCA S29031)

Cowell, Stanley "Prayer for Peace" (1972) on *Musa—Ancestral Streams* (Strata East SES 19743)

Dickerson, Walt "Universal Peace" and "Chant of Peace" (W. Dickerson) on *Peace* (NY: Inner City S-2042, 1975)

Evans, Bill "Peace Piece" (B. Evans, 1958) on: *Everybody Digs Bill Evans* (Riverside 291); *Peace Piece and Other Pieces* (Milestone M-47024, 1975)

Freeman, Chico "For the Peaceful Heart and the Gentle Spirit" (C. Freeman) on *Peaceful Heart, Gentle Spirit* (Contemporary 14005)

Goodman, Benny "Peace, Brother" on *Peace Brother/Darn That Dream* (NY: Columbia 35331, 1939)

Jamal, Ahmad "Peace at Last" (Colbert) on *Ahmad Jamal '73* (Twentieth Century 417)

Konitz, Lee "Peacemeal" (Katz) on *Peacemeal* (Milestone MLS 9025)

Lewis, George "Down by the Riverside" (Traditional) on *George Lewis and Turk Murphy at Newport* (Verve/Polygram UMV 2621, 1982)

Liebman, Dave "Troubled Peace" on Dave Liebman and Richard Beirach, *Forgotten Fantasies* (Horizon SP-709, 1975); Hiroshima Memorial (1983)

Lunceford, Jimmie "Peace and Love for All" (Corday) on *Jazz Heritage—Last Sparks*

(MCA S-1321, reissue of an original 1941 recording)

Mingus, Charles "O Lord Don't Let Them Drop That Atomic Bomb on Me" on *Oh Yeah* (Atlantic LP-1377, 1962)

————— "Prayer for Passive Resistance" (C. Mingus, 1960) on *Pre-Bird* (Limelight 1015, 1965) and on *Mingus at Antibes* (Atlantic 2-3001, 1976)

Muhammed, Idris "Peace and Rhythm Suite" (I. Muhammed) on *Peace and Rhythm* (Prestige 10036)

Murphy, Turk See G. Lewis

Ponty, Jean-Luc "Peace Crusaders" (J. L. Ponty) on *Civilized Evil* (Atlantic SD-16020, 1980)

Silver, Horace "Peace" (H. Silver) on *Blowin' the Blues Away* (Blue Note BLP 4017,1960s)

Smith, Willie the Lion "Peace on You" on *Peace on You/Noodlin'* (General 1712, 1930s)

Tyner, McCoy "Search for Peace" (M. Tyner) on *Passion Dance* (Milestone M-9091,1979)